TH
BIK

NORTHERN
CALIFORNIA

Strave
Map My Ride

THE BEST BIKE RIDES™ IN NORTHERN CALIFORNIA

Second Edition

by

Kimberly Grob

Revised by

John Elgart

The Globe Pequot Press

Old Saybrook, Connecticut

Cover photo: © Tony Stone Images/David Epperson
Photos by Kimberly Grob, Kevin Lee, Casey Mahone, Doug Simpkin-
son, and Seabreeze Photography

Library of Congress Cataloging-in-Publication Data
Grob, Kimberly.
   The best bike rides in Northern California / by Kimberly Grob; rev. John
Elgart. — 2nd ed.
       p.   cm.
   Rev. ed. of: The best bike rides in California. © 1995.
   Includes bibliographical references (p.).
   ISBN 0-7627-0126-9

   1. Bicycle touring—California, Northern—Guidebooks. 2. California,
Northern—Guidebooks. I. Elgart, John. II. Grob, Kimberly. Best bike rides
in California. III. Title.
 GV1045.5.C22C2548   1998

                                                    98-24361
                                                       CIP

To Kevin,

For always telling me I'm looking strong on long mountain climbs. Even when I'm ready to puke, topple over, or drop dead from exhaustion, you are always my faithful cheerleader.

Contents

Help Us Keep This Guide Up to Date

Every effort has been made by the author and editors to make this guide as accurate and useful as possible. However, many things can change after a guide is published—establishments close, phone numbers change, facilities come under new management, etc.

We would love to hear from you concerning your experiences with this guide and how you feel it could be made better and be kept up to date. While we may not be able to respond to all comments and suggestions, we'll take them to heart and we'll also make certain to share them with the author. Please send your comments and suggestions to the following address:

The Globe Pequot Press
Reader Response/Editorial Department
P.O. Box 833
Old Saybrook, CT 06475

Or you may e-mail us at:

editorial@globe-pequot.com

Thanks for your input, and happy travels!

Acknowledgments

This book could never have been written without the guidance and encouragement I've received from family, friends, industry peers, and, often, strangers. Thanks to my first editor at *California Bicyclist,* Dave Butler, for getting me involved in this highly addictive sport, and to Phrancis Falcone for taking me on my first real ride. Thanks also to *California Bicyclist's* Henry Kingman for sharing his abundant knowledge of California backroads and for recommending me for this book project. Furthermore, I'm grateful to Nancy Vierra, Sheri Pepper, and Linda Rosek for allowing me the flexibility in my part-time job to get this project completed. And I'm forever grateful to my parents and my sisters, Jennifer and Amy, for their sympathetic ears, to all my close friends who have been neglected during the writing of this book, and to Kevin Lee for accompanying me on many a road ride when he would have preferred to be somewhere else.

Many cyclists have contributed rides to this book. Some of them are friends that merely took me on a mind-blowing ride years back, never knowing it would one day be incorporated in a book. Others are acquaintances and strangers who've been willing to share some of their favorite rides specifically for this book. Those cyclists include Ernst Wilhelm, Stefan Klakovich, Dale Butler, Henry Kingman, Barbara Hanscome, Andrew Christensen, Chris Kostman, Bob Winning, Ed McLaughlin, Patrick Owens, Monica Pappas, Kathy Enquist, Joe Zoellin, and Larry Tubbs. Thanks also to many helpful strangers who pointed me in the right direction and gave me a helping hand out on the road in times of trouble. If you ride your bike long enough, you will learn that there are plenty of Good Samaritans left in the world. Thanks to all of them, whose names I never got the chance to learn.

Acknowledgments to the Second Edition:

I'd like to thank the many cyclists who contributed material for the second edition: Linda Elgart for research and proofing the text; Ron Jones, interpretative ranger, Humboldt Redwoods State Park; the staff at Los Padres National Forest; Will Spurling, Henderson Center Bicycles, Eureka; Rod Olson, The Mountain Peddler, Angels Camp; Sara Brown, Bike Lane, Chico; Alpine County Chamber of Commerce; Petaluma Chamber of Commerce; Mark Tarasco, Baywood Cyclery, Los Ossos; the staff at Art's Cyclery, San Luis Obispo; the staff at Sunstorm Cyclery, Paso Robles; Ophie Chavez, Winning Wheels, Pacific Grove; Bill Oetinger, Santa Rosa Cycling Club; Steve Wryostok of the Bikadelic Bikestore and Espresso Cafe, Fairfax; Henry Kingman; Dave Stahl of Alto Velo; Allen King of Bike and Ski Sports, Minden, NV; Chris Espy of Bicycles Plus in Folsom; Larry Robinson of The Rest Stop, Sacramento; Carter Schmeck of Bicycle Emporium in Auburn; Mike Bohn of Gianni Cyclery, Occidental.

Introduction

Ride your bike, even if it fails to draw admiring glances at the post-ride cafe. Even if the self you see in your fantasies wouldn't be seen on it. The ride's the thing.
— Maynard Hershon, *California Bicyclist*

When you're nine years old, bicycling isn't a route slip and a map, and it certainly isn't a titanium stem or hand-built wheels. It's a blur of colors. A rush of wind. A feeling of freedom. Kids don't need much of anything to enjoy the sport, except their own self-reliance and thirst for adventure. It's a time in life when riding is as pure as it gets. But eventually we grow up and things get more complicated. We buy nicer bikes. We buy touring books.

In 1976 I entered my first bicycle race. Freckled and flat-chested and toothpick-legged, I shoved my way up to the front of the start line with the older boys. As the start drew near, my legs twitched with nervous energy. My face flushed hot with anxiety. Six miles through the subdivision to the swimming pool and back. I'd done it a million times. One-handed. No-handed. Pedaling with Sheryl Mixon on the seat and Little Lynn on the handlebars. I could do it now. And I could win. Because I was nine and I was a girl and I knew how strong I was; the anvil of gender hadn't yet been dropped on me.

The race started, and I spun glorious, joyous, girlish pedalstrokes amid the neighborhood boys twice my age. But little more than 100 yards from the start line, my glory ride ended in a heap of metal and tears and twisted limbs. A boy—out of control in the frenzy of competition—barreled into me, abruptly finishing the ride for both of us.

I didn't think about bikes again for thirteen years, and it was seventeen years before I tried another race. Instead, I busied myself with the normal girl things. I took gymnastics and ballet. I wrote

boys' names on my Trapper Keeper. I went to the prom. I went to college. I grew up to be a Very Nice Girl. And while there was almost always a bike in my life during those years, I don't remember any of them; they were either gathering dust in a garage or getting rusted in the rain.

I remember instead a blue bike with fenders, ordered for me from the Sears catalog: the dented, rattling, squeaky steed of my ill-fated ride of 1976. I remember my pride in the "Spirit of '76" logo I stenciled on the chain guard with red spray paint, just to be fancy. And I remember the giddy rush of riding as fast as I could through soft, wooded dirt on early summer mornings. Cars and houses and neighborhood kids gone, I was a little girl alone, zooming past tall, damp trees. And it was frightening and fun and free.

That bike must've cost my parents $50, tops. It was just a cheap, department-store thing. It wasn't for racing, and it wasn't for mountain biking. But I didn't know that, so on it I did both. On it I rode like a little girl who hasn't yet learned to be prissy. Like any reckless kid—boy or girl—who hasn't discovered fear. Fear of accidents, insurance premiums, and equipment. Fear of having a bike that's too heavy, too cheap, too ugly, too embarrassing—generally not right.

My Spirit of '76 bike is long gone. But even now, sometimes, when everything is going right and I'm riding strong and confident and energetic, that giddy, girlish feeling I used to get when I mounted the Spirit of '76 comes back to me. For a moment the fears of adulthood are washed away, not by titanium or clipless pedals or aero bars but by the unfathomable beauty of a California ridge, the wind in my face on a coasty, twisty descent, or the pure, breathless exhaustion of an all-out sprint—whether racing against strangers or on a bike path with friends.

Use this book as a tool to help you get to that place—if only for a moment—where bicycling is as good and pure as it was when you were a kid. You can be a formidable racer, or you can be slower than your grandpa on his John Deere tractor; your bike can cost a conservative $200, or it can cost a cool $2,000. But if you're out there riding long enough, it'll get you there. And it won't matter that you have a mortgage payment due and an insurance policy to worry about. Or that your bike doesn't sport the latest gadget. For the moment, all that will matter is that you're on your bike and you're alive and you're lucky enough to be riding in California, one of the most dramatic and diverse states in all of America.

Enjoy the rides!

How to Use This Book

Think of this book as an old, weathered cycling friend. The one who's been around the proverbial block more than a few times. This buddy of yours will take you on a sampling of its favorite rides, but in the long run you'll find your own variations of these, and you'll come up with your own list of favorites.

By all means, branch out! This book is not a bible; it's merely a starting point, a launching pad for your own adventures. It's meant to be a trusty resource, an accurate, reliable guide, and a faithful friend. But those who get the most out of its pages will be those who are bold enough to build upon the book's suggestions.

For starters, each time you embark on one of these rides, it's a good idea to carry a road map of the area in addition to the map appearing in this book. That way you'll be able to navigate around unexpected road construction, get yourself out of a pickle if you become totally lost, and discover new roads to ride. There are some great cycling-specific maps produced by Krebs Cycle Products that highlight scenic roads and make it easy to chart your own routes and find those elusive backroads. (For more information on this and other resources, see the Appendixes in the back of this book.)

In order to arm you with the knowledge you'll need to get the most out of this book, every ride is rated to reflect its degree of difficulty.

Rambles are the gentlest rides, perfect for the beginning cyclist or for riders looking for a relaxed outing. All rambles are less than 30 miles long and cover flat or rolling terrain.

Cruises are intermediate-level rides, ranging in length from 25 to 60 miles. They include rolling hills and sometimes a major climb.

Challenges require more experience. Beginning riders who take on challenges may find themselves cursing the road, this book, and life in general about halfway through the ride. These routes are tough. They're often longer than 60 miles. They always include major climbs. They make your legs hurt.

Classics are the most difficult rides in the book and are most suitable for experienced riders. They are usually more than 75 miles, sometimes more than 100, and they always include tough climbs. Tackle them at your own risk, and don't say I didn't warn you!

The rating system is designed to help you choose rides that are appropriate for your experience level, riding style, and mood for the day. Feel like trying to lure your nonbikie friend into the sport? An ultrascenic ramble may be just the ticket. Experiencing the need to hammer your brains out and restate your virility? There are classics in here that could frighten even the most bad-assed, big-legged bike fanatics around. Of course, most of the rides are somewhere in between these two extremes, and many of them are doable by just about anyone. So take these ratings as suggestions, and try not to get too hung up on the definitions. A ramble may seem more like a classic to a beginner, and the real toughsters out there may laugh at some of the rides I call challenges.

Getting the Most Out of Your Ride

Think of all the cyclo-journalists out there who have penned articles, papers, and books on our many-faceted sport. Just on the subject of smart and safe riding techniques, stacks of articles and books have been written. And while collecting and absorbing written advice can improve your riding tremendously, it's the miles in the saddle that really make the cyclist. Learning to ride intelligently—and to ride with grace, etiquette, and class—is a continual process of education and experience. It seems there's always more to learn.

Cyclo-journalists and their cycling advice have been around since the invention of two wheels. There is, however, at least a common thread in their teachings. The following cycling credo was developed in the late 1800s by a respected writer and rider named Velocio (Paul de Vivie). It covers all the basics and is as relevant today as it was then.

Velocio's Commandments

1. Stop briefly and not too often, so as not to chill or lose your rhythm.
2. Eat frequently and lightly, eat before you are hungry, and drink before you are thirsty.
3. Don't push yourself until you're too tired to eat or sleep.
4. Add clothing before you are cold, take it off before you are hot, but don't avoid sun, air, and rain.
5. Avoid alcohol and meat, at least while on the road.
6. Ride within your limits. Learn your pace, and don't be tempted to force yourself during the first hours of a ride, when you are fresh.
7. Don't show off (ride out of vanity).

To this I add a 1990s addendum: Always wear a helmet.

For more cycling resources that'll move you forward in your quest to be a safe and smart rider, check out the Appendixes in the back of this book.

Disclaimer

The Globe Pequot Press assumes no liability for accidents happening to, or injuries sustained by, readers who engage in the activities described in this book.

Upper North

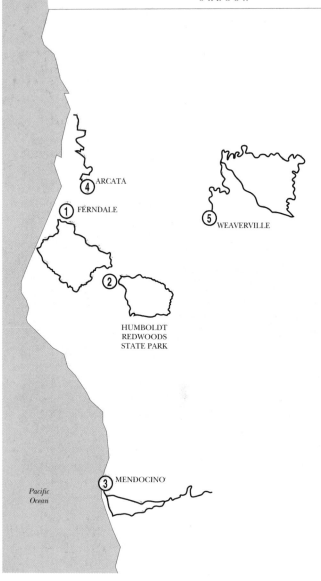

OREGON

④ ARCATA

① FERNDALE

②

HUMBOLDT
REDWOODS
STATE PARK

⑤ WEAVERVILLE

③ MENDOCINO

Pacific
Ocean

Upper North

1

Lost Coast Classic

Ferndale—Scotia—Avenue of the Giants—Honey-dew—Petrolia—Lost Coast—Capetown—Ferndale

> *After 80 miles, if the road rises at all, it rises near-vertically. At least once, no matter how long you've been riding, you'll reach for low gear as eagerly as a drowning man reaches for a lifesaving rope—and already be in it. Gulp.*
> —Maynard Hershon, *California Bicyclist*

Hanging precipitously on the edge of California, the Lost Coast is like a chaste beauty living in an ivory tower. Despite its eye-popping splendor, the inaccessibility of the land locks it into virtual anonymity. When Highway 101 turns inward at Legget, it takes with it the majority of auto-addicted tourists. Only the most intrepid of travelers, the ones who can handle not having a major highway or city anywhere nearby, make it to the isolated shores of the Lost Coast. Because of this, the area is ideal for cycling. The secluded backroads that make up this ride range from dense, dark redwood groves to a jagged coastline of black-sand beaches stretching out to meet the Pacific Ocean.

The ride takes you almost 75 miles before your wheels actually roll onto the Lost Coast Road. For the sake of convenience, the ride starts at an accessible locale and gets progressively "lost" with every mile. The Victorian hamlet of Ferndale, which boasts painted-lady homes and elegant storefronts decorated in pastels and fancy trim work, is the starting point for the ride. The town's ornamental charm is in ultimate contrast to the unrestrained beauty of the Lost Coast.

This route is patterned after the annual Tour of the Unknown Coast century ride, which is touted as one of California's toughest centuries. And after eight miles of cycling, you'll get a taste of what you're in for when you encounter your first big hill en route to Rio Dell. From here, it's a short ride to Scotia, a town almost completely owned by Pacific Lumber Company. This lumber empire extends from one end of town to the other, and when you finally roll to the end of it, you'll turn onto Highway 101S.

As you pedal onto Highway 101, your ability to measure your progress in small chunks from city to city all but disappears. After nearly six miles, you'll leave the rush of cars behind and greet the ancient redwoods as you pedal onto the famed Avenue of the Giants. The soft, dank shelter of these towering trees yields a mossy carpet of forest floor, with mushrooms sprouting everywhere in a wild, mutating frenzy.

A good side trip at this point is to visit Founder's Grove, which is 300 yards beyond the turnoff for Bull Creek Road. The Dyerville Giant, once the world's tallest tree, but now fallen, is worth a visit.

Your route tumbles deeper into the secluded world of nature as you turn onto Bull Creek Road and begin a gentle, quiet climb through the redwoods. The road is a pastoral poem where sheep roam freely, often holding court right in the middle of the road.

When you reach the tiny town of Honeydew, at mile 55.6, you'll find a store where you can refuel and chill out for a while. From here, country roads transport you through the town of Petrolia, which also has a store, and finally deposit you at the Lost Coast. And it is here, at mile 73, that much hardship awaits.

At the coast, particularly in the afternoon, gusty winds laced with sand can drop your cruising speed down to less than 10 mph. Cattle wandering aimlessly along the road provide that obstacle-course element so often missing in other rides. And then there's The Wall. At mile 81.5, your wind-beaten limbs will be forced to attack a 1-mile, 18 percent grade. And right after you've recovered from that, you'll be faced with the Endless Hill, thrown in for good measure at mile 86.7, just to ensure that you've really worked for your 100 miles. After 85 miles of pedaling, a bump on the road can seem endless—and this 8-mile climb ain't no bump.

Just remember, when you reach the summit, you're finally home free. A swooshing, spiraling descent drops you back into Ferndale, and leaves you finishing the ride with the perfect combination of feelings: accomplishment for riding 100 miles and exhilaration for getting to end them with a thrilling descent.

The Basics

Start: Intersection of Ocean St. and Main St. in downtown Ferndale.

Length: 100 miles.

Terrain: Three extended climbs, many rolling hills, heavy winds with gusts of sand on coast. Temperatures can vary dramatically, so dress in layers.

Food: You can get a good breakfast in Ferndale, right on Main Street. There are stores in Honeydew and Petrolia where you can buy some snacks for lunch and stock up on food to carry you through the day. Back in Ferndale, treat yourself to a heaping big meal.

For more information: Henderson Center Bicycle, 2811 F St., Eureka, CA, 95501; (707) 443–9861.

Miles & Directions

- 0.0 South on Ocean St. at the intersection of Ocean and Main in Ferndale.

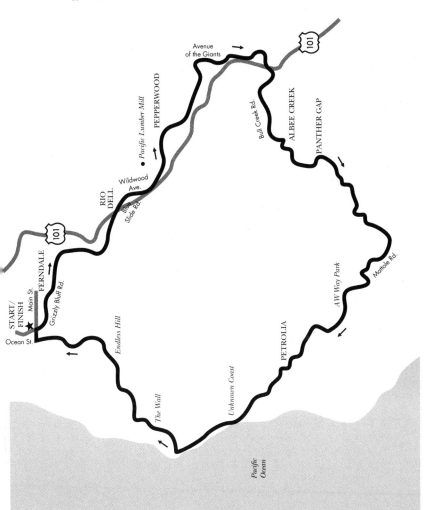

- 3.7 Straight past Waddington Rd.; Ocean St. becomes Grizzly Bluff Rd.
- 5.4 Pass Grizzly Bluff School
- 13.1 Grizzly Bluff Rd. becomes Blue Slide Rd.; descend into Rio Dell. Right onto Wildwood Ave.
- 14.4 Scotia. Pass Pacific Lumber Mill.
- 15.9 Enter Hwy. 101S. Yes, this is a legal bike route!
- 21.7 Exit Hwy. 101 at Pepperwood. Left at stop sign onto Avenue of the Giants.
- 31.7 Right onto Bull Creek Rd./Honeydew exit under 101.
- 38.0 Albee Creek.
- 46.7 Begin ascent of Panther Gap.
- 48.3 Summit. Be careful on the twisty descent.
- 53.0 Honeydew. Right on Mattole Rd.
- 63.0 AW Way Park, a county campground.
- 69.0 Petrolia. Stay on paved road through town.
- 73.0 Unknown Coast.
- 81.5 Begin ascent of The Wall; 18 percent grade.
- 82.5 Summit. Descend to Capetown at the Bear River.
- 86.7 Begin climb of the Endless Hill.
- 96.0 Summit.
- 100.0 Sharp right at bottom of Wildcat Grade. Ride ends at Ocean and Main Sts. in Ferndale.

2

Dyerville Loop Challenge

*Founders' Grove—Dyerville Loop Road—Humboldt
Redwoods State Park—Avenue of the Giants—Myers
Flat—Weott—Founders' Grove*

> *Is it anaerobic agony or endorphin ecstasy? Sheer lunacy
> or athletic artistry?*
> —Barbara Hanscome, *California Bicyclist*

It is said that the legendary Bigfoot, monstrous icon of the far-
out 1970s, has been routinely spotted in the wilds of Humboldt
County and Humboldt Redwoods State Park. And on your bike,
alone, in the solitude of an untamed forest, it's easy to shelve
your jaded 1990s sensibility and embrace a world where fairies,
gnomes, and even Bigfoot roam freely, ready to pop out from
around the next corner.

There are times on the Dyerville Loop Challenge that anything seems possible. In between the few clusters of homes that
could loosely be called towns, the ride is eerily quiet. In wet,
deep green forests, ancestral redwoods stand stoic and unyielding: thousands of stories to tell, thousands of secrets kept. Out
of the woodlands the Eel River snakes gently through open pasturelands where skinny-armed trees wave psychedelically from
shimmery green branches. Roads climb abruptly to nowhere,
only to drop back down again. And on this ride life presents itself as creepily mystical, uncanny, fantastic.

Although this loop ride is only 23 miles, there are many reasons to deem it a challenge. You'll immediately leave the flat, cool forest of Humboldt Redwoods State Park for the warmer, open fields of the surrounding area, so dress in layers; you won't want that long-sleeved jersey for more than a few miles. The roads are steep and rough for the first 9 miles, and the steepest and longest of the many climbs charges up a dirt and gravel fire road. With its steep switchbacks and numerous false summits, this unrelenting road does its best to defeat even the most intrepid of road bikers. To make it easier try wider tires if your bike will allow for them. Or bring a mountain bike or hybrid; the ride is short enough that it can be done comfortably on just about any bike as long as it has a wide gear ratio.

As you near the summit of this grand climb, the grade mellows out a bit, and with your nose out of the proverbial grindstone, you're free to loop up, wipe the sweat from your brow, and see where your legs have take you. Beyond the dense trees that from a cool canopy above, you'll see glimpses of far-off, snow-covered peaks, as well as the Eel River, tiny now and far below.

High above the tall redwoods and state park tourists, this virtually carless road summits at a small community of modest homes, many of which are little more than dilapidated shacks with washing machines and the like piled up on sagging porches. There are no stores. No gas stations. No schools. Just small farms and clusters of country mailboxes with Dyerville Loop Road addresses.

You are in the middle of nowhere, yet only 5 miles away from the security of organized nature at Humboldt Redwoods State Park and the famed Avenue of the Giants. As you drop down Elk Creek Road back to the park, notice the dramatic terrain change from rolling, hilltop pastures to the lush valley of the redwood groves.

The flat terrain of the Avenue of the Giants is a gorgeous reprieve from the steep grades of Dyerville Loop and Elk Creek Roads. The cool camp air massages your burning quads, and on the Avenue of the Giants, you're back to being a tourist again, leaving the rugged-adventurer stuff far behind on that gnarly dirt road. This comfort, however, brings a compromise: The Avenue of the Giants can be rather trafficky, making it best to plan your ride in the spring or fall, before the droves of Winnebagos descend. On your bike, it's easy to make impromptu stops on the Avenue of the Giants to enjoy the dank, dark redwood groves. You also can drop in on the small but impressive visitor center, check out the eccentric locals, or stop for snack in Myers Flat, or just head back to the ride's start and finish at Founders' Grove. Here you can peel off your biking shoes, don your hiking boots, and take a short and easy hike on the Founders' Grove nature trail to stretch out your legs and soak up the wonder of the natural world.

The Basics

Start: Founders' Grove, on the Avenue of the Giants, in Humboldt Redwoods State Park.
Length: 23 miles.
Terrain: Steep, extended climbing. Rough roads; 2.2 miles of climbing on dirt and gravel road. Little to no traffic on Dyerville Loop Rd. and Elk Creek Rd. Weekend and tourist traffic on Avenue of the Giants.
Food: Two diners and a general store are located in Myers Flat.
For more information: Humboldt Redwoods State Park, P.O. Box 100, Weott, CA 95571; (707) 946–2409.

Miles & Directions

- 0.0 East or left onto Dyerville Loop Rd. from Founders' Grove parking lot.
- 0.5 Leave Humboldt Redwoods State Park.
- 0.6 Begin climb.
- 1.5 Summit.
- 2.2 Ride under subway; pass Redwood Area Seventh-Day Adventist Church.

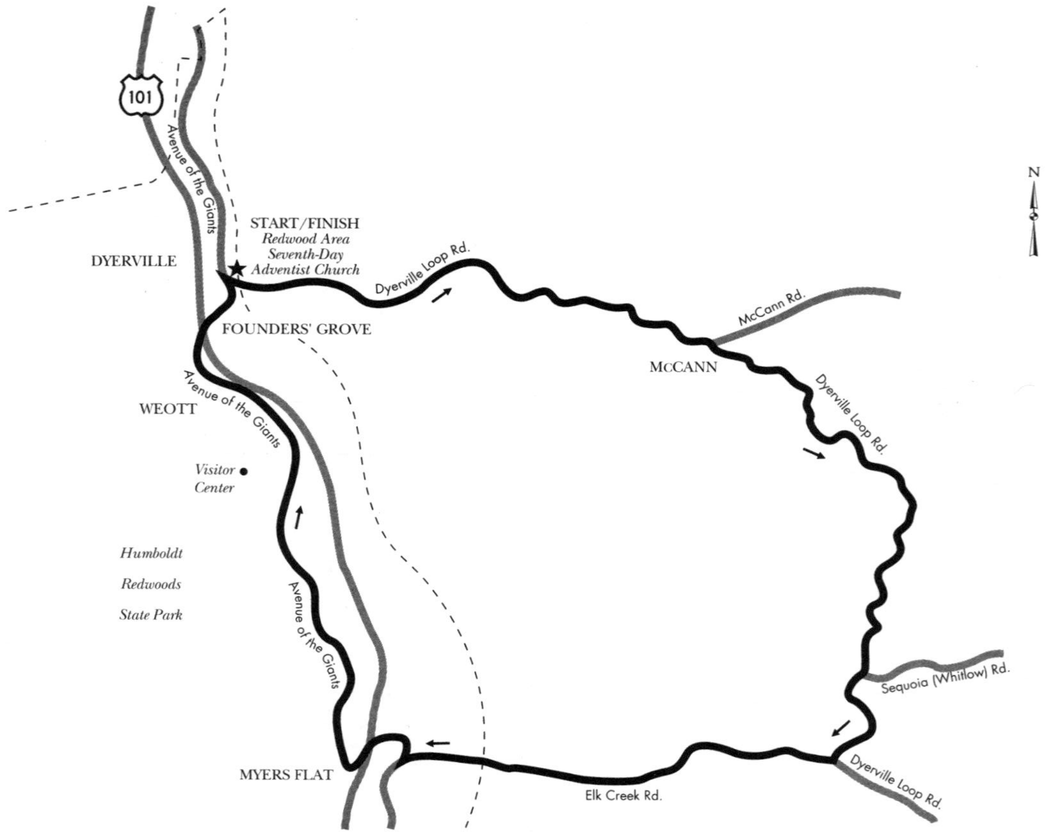

N

McCann Rd.

Dyerville Loop Rd.

Sequoia (Whitlow) Rd.

Dyerville Loop Rd.

McCANN

Elk Creek Rd.

Dyerville Loop Rd.

START/FINISH
Redwood Area
Seventh-Day
Adventist Church

FOUNDERS' GROVE

Avenue of the Giants

Avenue of the Giants

MYERS FLAT

WEOTT

Visitor
Center

Avenue of the Giants

DYERVILLE

Humboldt
Redwoods
State Park

101

- 3.7 Cross railroad track; begin climb.
- 4.7 Summit.
- 6.5 Dyerville Loop Rd. intersects with McCann Rd.; continue straight on Dyerville Loop Rd.
- 6.7 Cross railroad track. Dyerville Loop Rd. turns to dirt. Begin steep climb.
- 8.9 Summit at Sequoia (Whitlow) Rd. Continue straight on Dyerville Loop Rd.
- 10.0 Right onto Elk Creek Rd. Follow sign that says HWY. 101 5 MILES.
- 12.8 Right onto Avenue of the Giants at the stop sign.
- 14.6 Myers Flat. Rider under 101N.
- 18.8 Humboldt Redwoods State Park visitor center.
- 20.4 Weott.
- 20.7 Hike & Bike Camp.
- 22.8 Right at Founders' Grove.
- 23.0 Ride ends at Founders' Grove parking lot.

3

Comptche Cruise

Mendocino—Little River—Van Damme State Park
Pygmy Forest—Comptche—Mendocino

I shall be telling this with a sigh/Somewhere ages and ages hence:/Two roads diverged in a wood, and I—/I took the one less traveled by,/And that has made all the difference.

—Robert Frost, "The Road Not Taken"

Highway 1 curls groggily into the misty oceanside town of Mendocino. From the distance the town looks tiny and sleepy as it lunges forth from the highway, jutting out on a rocky, jagged edge to meet the Pacific Ocean. A closer inspection, however, reveals a lot of tourist-driven cheesiness behind the town's charming New England facade. Yet despite its unabashed commercialism, Mendocino *is*—dare I say it?—cute. But where do you draw the line between cuteness and gaudiness? How long can you shop? How many driftwood clocks and paintings of whales can you look at?

This, of course, is why you have a bike. The magic of Mendocino lies outside its city limits and simply cannot be properly appreciated or explored within the confines of an automobile. From its rocky coast to its densely forested inland mountains, Mendocino County is perhaps the most dramatically beautiful county in all of California. And the quiet country roads leading to middle-of-nowhere towns provide a brief glimpse into the lives of random town residents from all kinds of backgrounds.

Stop for a minute and listen to their stories: They'll happily tell you how they count their blessings daily for being fortunate enough to have all this unadulterated peacefulness right in their backyards.

The Comptche Cruise begins by exiting historic (hysteric?) downtown Mendocino and heading south on the twisty, turny, drop-off-the-face-of-the-earth Highway 1. After 3 miles of riding past oceanside resorts and B&Bs, you'll hit the unassuming Little River Road. This is the kind of road that immediately makes your lips curl upward, because you know, just by looking at the arching trees above it and the way it rambles off to nowhere special, that you've found a killer backroad, the kind of road that cyclists love and car drivers hate.

After less than 3 miles on Little River Road, you'll come to the Van Damme State Park Pygmy Forest—a place that lives up to its intriguing name and is well worth a quick look. A raised wooden walkway twists and turns in a maniacal maze through decades-old trees that stand no taller than 4 feet because of the highly acidic soil content and poor drainage.

At the end of Little River Road, you reach the beginning of Comptche-Ukiah Road. There may be no sign to tell you what road you're on or where it leads to, but turn right and you'll be heading for Comptche, which is another 9 miles of near-orgasmic cycling away. The Comptche-Ukiah Road is cut into the side of a mountain with a severe dropoff to the redwood valleys far below it. To the left your backdrop is an unending horizon of tree-covered mountains, dreamily softened by the fog that often hovers at their tops. To the right a lush wall of damp, thick forest hugs the side of the road.

After you have cycled only a few miles on this glorious road's summit, the road swoops downward to Comptche. Four miles of descending carries you out of the forested woodlands and into the open grasslands, complete with small farms and houses, lazy cows and sheep. From here it's 5 relatively flat miles to the booming metropolis of Comptche, featuring one post office, one store with gas station, one church, and one school. Stop for a snack at the market and relax with the

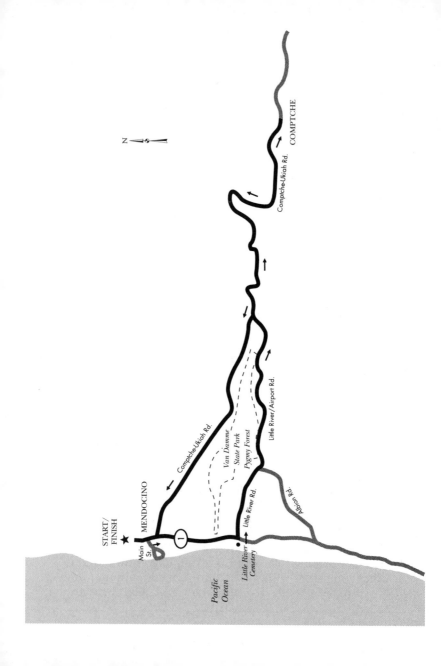

Comptche locals, who can often be found hanging out on the one bench in front of the one store.

Incidentally, the Comptche-Ukiah Road is now paved all the way to Ukiah, an additional 70 miles round-trip.

This is a turnaround point, so fuel up for the extended climb back on Comptche-Ukiah Road. This long, gradual ascent provides the same forested vistas but from an opposite—and much slower—perspective. When you get to Little River Road, continue straight on Comptche-Ukiah for a fast and easy descent offering awe-inspiring views of the Pacific Ocean and Mendocino. It's a great payback for all the climbing and a perfect way to end a ride.

Back on Highway 1, you're less than 1 mile away from Mendocino. And after a hearty day of backroads cycling, it's easier to justify one's inherent American urge to indulge in the consumer orgy—so get off your bike, visit town, and eat, drink, and shop to your heart's content.

The Basics

Start: Mendocino, at the intersection of Main St. and Hwy. 1.
Length: 32.9 miles.
Terrain: One major climb, some rollers, lengthy flat stretches on quiet backroads.
Food: Health-food markets and all sorts of restaurants in Mendocino; one small store in Comptche.
For more information: Catch a Canoe & Bicycles, Too! at The Stanford Inn by the Sea, Hwy. 1 at Comptche-Ukiah Rd., Mendocino; (707) 937–0273. Bicycle rentals available. The Mendocino Coast is an area where you may want to bring your mountain bike. Nearby Jackson State Forest has abundant trails and is now open to bicycles.

Miles & Directions

- 0.0 Right onto Hwy. 1 at the intersection of Hwy. 1 and Main St. in Mendocino. Traffic here is usually heavy during tourist season.
- 3.1 Left onto Little River/Airport Rd., immediately past Little River Cemetery.
- 5.8 Van Damme State Park Pygmy Forest to the left, Albion Rd. to the right. Continue straight on Little River Rd.
- 9.0 Little River Rd. Ts at a possibly unmarked road, which is Comptche-Ukiah Rd. Turn right. Traffic on Comptche-Ukiah is fairly light, though there are occasional logging trucks.
- 18.0 Comptche. Turnaround point.
- 26.1 Intersect with Little River Rd.; continue straight on Comptche-Ukiah Rd.
- 32.3 Comptche-Ukiah Rd. Ts at Hwy. 1. Turn right.
- 32.9 Ride ends at intersection of Hwy. 1 and Main St. in Mendocino.

4

Patrick's Point Cruise

Arcata—Clam Beach State Park—Trinidad—
Patrick's Point—Arcata

> *If you give it an inch—Nay, a hair—it will take a yard*
> *—Nay, an evolution—And give you a contusion, or,*
> *like enough, a perforated kneecap.*
>
> —Francis E. Willard,
> *How I Learned to Ride the Bicycle*

On a misty gray day in the North Coast town of Arcata, when the chill seeps right through to your bones, straddling a cold metal bike is just about as appealing as skinny-dipping in the Arctic Circle. Even in the summer, frigid fog can hang over the coast for most of the morning, creating an overcast mood that leads to lingering over coffee, reading the paper in pajamas, analyzing cloud formations for signs of rain—anything but suiting up in Lycra and slinging your leg over a top tube.

Problem is, waiting for sunshine often means sacrificing a good part of your day. So cyclists in Arcata have learned to adapt. You'll see them out there—rain or shine—with fenders on their bikes, waterproof windbreakers on their backs, and layers of bike clothing ready to be peeled off at the first sight of sunshine. And if you're able to muster up enough internal willpower to get out there and join them, you'll realize they aren't just enduring the weather—they're actually enjoying it.

The Patrick's Point Cruise is a favorite local out-and-back that provides dramatic views of the jagged North Coast, including 3 miles of windswept coastal riding on a stretch of road that seems poised on the edge of the earth and ready to crumble into the Pacific Ocean at any moment.

The ride starts at Wildberries Marketplace, 13th and G Streets, in downtown Arcata, a gently accepting type of town where the macrobiotic-diet crowd (intelligentsia from Humboldt State University) mixes easily with the meat-and-potatoes crowd (farming and lumber-industry families who've lived here all their lives). Two miles out of Arcata, the flat and fast roads become increasingly rural; houses are separated by large plots of farmland where cows graze loosely in wide-open fields. The voluptuous curves of Mad River Road eventually lead to the river, where an arched bike and pedestrian bridge links recreation seekers to the Hammond Bike Path. A well-traveled throughway, this route connects Mad River Park with Hiller Park and, eventually, the ocean.

The bike path ends 0.5 mile from Highway 101N, which is perfectly legal for bikes and only moderately trafficky (as well as being the only road north). You can, however, avoid a good deal of it by exiting at Clam Beach State Park, where you can ride alongside sandy dunes instead of smoggy cars. At the end of the park road, you'll have approximately 1.5 miles of highway to endure, including crossing a short bridge with no shoulder and hauling yourself up the ride's only extended climb (less than 0.5 mile) to the Westhaven Drive exit.

From here the slight Scenic Drive winds bold and treacherous above the Pacific, clinging to the edge of a rocky cliff for dear life. For motorists it may be a white-knuckle drive, but for cyclists it's nothing short of cathartic. Below the road, waves roll in to massage the craggy sand. In the distance Patrick's Point juts abruptly out from land toward ocean, standing triumphantly and defiantly above the waves that crash around it.

A rolling 5 miles on Patrick's Point Road, thick with trees and intermittent coastal views, brings you to the entrance of

Patrick's Point State Park. But it's 1 mile farther to the *actual* Patrick's Point, which stands more than 200 feet above the ocean and provides unsurpassed views of the rocky, misty, stoically beautiful North Coast. Excursions to Patrick's Point, which is often much colder than the rest of the park due to bitter winds, usually require putting on that windbreaker you've had stuffed in your jersey pocket for the last 15 miles.

If you're finding it hard to tear yourself away, the cold air may serve as the final catalyst to get you back on your bike. From the park just reverse directions and head back in the opposite way toward Arcata. Your return trip may be aided if you think beer. When the ride ends in Arcata, you'll be less than 0.5 mile from the center of town, where a hearty micro-brewed beer awaits at the award-winning Humboldt Brewery.

The Basics

Start: Wildberries Marketplace, 13th and G Sts. in downtown Arcata.

Length: 46 miles.

Terrain: Mostly flat, with a few rolling hills and one extended climb; 4 miles of moderately trafficked highway riding.

Food: Best bet for food is Arcata. Wildberries is a good source for healthy snacks you can pack in your jersey for the ride. There's a small store 6 miles into the ride at the intersection of School Rd. Also, you can purchase picnic foods and deli sandwiches at the large grocery store in Trinidad, just 5 miles from Patrick's Point, where Scenic Dr. becomes Patrick's Point Rd.

For more information: Henderson Center Bike Shop, 2811 F St., Eureka, CA 95501; (701) 443–7827. Revolution Bicycle Repair, 1360 G St., Arcata, CA 95521; (707) 822–2562.

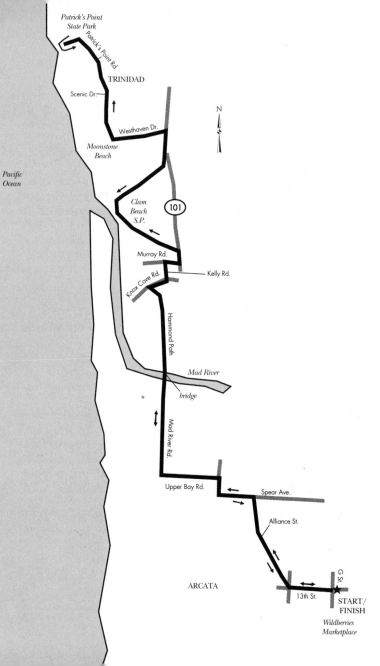

Patrick's Point
State Park

Patrick's Point Rd.

TRINIDAD

Scenic Dr.

Westhaven Dr.

Moonstone
Beach

Pacific
Ocean

N

Clam
Beach
S.P.

101

Murray Rd.

Knox Cove Rd. ——— Kelly Rd.

Hammond Path

Mad River

bridge

Mad River Rd.

Upper Bay Rd.   Spear Ave.

Alliance St.

ARCATA   G St.

13th St.   START/
                FINISH

Wildberries
Marketplace

Miles & Directions

- 0.0 Left onto 13th at 13th and G Sts.
- 0.4 Right onto Alliance St.
- 1.5 Left onto Spear Ave.
- 2.1 Left onto Upper Bay Rd. across from Pacific Union School.
- 2.8 Right onto Mad River Rd.
- 5.3 Right onto bike/pedestrian bridge marked HAMMOND TRAIL/COASTAL TRAIL.
- 6.4 Veer onto Hammond Bike Path.
- 6.6 Continue on bike path into Hiller Park.
- 7.4 Pacific Ocean. Right onto Knox Cove Rd.
- 7.5 Left onto Kelly Rd.
- 7.6 Right at road's end onto Murray Rd.
- 8.0 Left onto 101N toward Crescent City.
- 10.4 Exit 101N at Clam Beach State Park.
- 10.6 Left on Clam Beach.
- 12.1 Cross 101 overpass. Left on 101N.
- 12.6 *Caution!* Cross short bridge on 101 with no shoulder.
- 12.9 Begin climb.
- 13.3 Summit at Westhaven Dr.; exit at Westhaven Dr.
- 13.5 Left to Moonstone Beach, then right onto Scenic Dr.
- 16.8 Trinidad. Scenic Dr. becomes Patrick's Point Rd.
- 22.1 Left into Patrick's Point State Park.
- 23.0 Patrick's Point. Turnaround point.

* Return following the same route, with two notes: Exit 101S at Little River Beach (by the weigh station) for the Clam Beach stretch that temporarily gets you off the highway. Get off 101 for good at the Murray Rd. exit. You'll reach a sign that says NOT A THROUGH ROAD, but continue on—it does take you to the Hammond Bike Path.

5

Trinity Alps Challenge

*Weaverville—Whiskeytown-Shasta-Trinity
National Recreation Area—Trinity Lake—
Lewiston—Weaverville*

*Never measure the height of a mountain until you have
reached the top. Then you will see how low it was.*
—Dag Hammarskjöld, former UN
secretary-general, *Markings*

Tucked into the folds of Highway 299's mountainous undulations, the town of Weaverville stands as a slight bit of civilization encircled by Trinity County's 3,220 square miles of rushing rivers, snowy peaks, expansive lakes, and protected wilderness areas. Relatively unchanged from its historic mining days, the town features wooden sidewalks and balconies that give it an Old West feel; one look around town and you can't help but ponder the round-and-tumble lives of California's first settlers.

But get on your bike and pedal just a few miles away from this sleepy hamlet and another history unfolds. The Trinity Alps mountains—ancestral predecessors to Weaverville, mining, and humankind—have their own stories to tell. And grinding up the side of one of their ridges on your bike is just the way to listen to what these mountains have to say.

The Trinity Alps Challenge immediately departs town and heads for Shasta-Trinity State Park and the Whiskeytown-Shasta-Trinity National Recreation Area, where one climb leads to another climb leads to another climb until you are high above sprawling Trinity Lake and dizzy with adrenaline. From the summit of Trinity Dam Boulevard, white jagged peaks cradle the tiny mountaintop road with all the power and precariousness of an unpredictable giant.

Here all your climbing pays off in the form of a long, steep descent. As you drop down to Trinity Lake, you'll have less of an opportunity to enjoy the natural beauty of your surroundings but more of a chance to revel in the pure thrill of plummeting down a fast mountain road. At the bottom of the descent, you get a bit of a reprieve from all the previous ups and downs as you ride along the base of the lake, where campgrounds, boat launches, and fishing camps dot your path.

A 1-mile climb out of the Whiskeytown-Shasta-Trinity Recreation Area marks the outskirts of Lewiston. Another historic mining town, this curious little settlement crops up spontaneously and is just as quickly engulfed by wilderness. The small town forms a tiny sanctuary from the forested wilds of the Trinity Alps and consists of an original Old West hotel, a few antiques shops, a B&B, and little else.

From Lewiston the ride back to Weaverville follows Rush Creek Road, a lightly traveled route with sporadic country homes hidden behind walls of trees. There's one more extended climb that lasts for only 1 mile but seems endless—perhaps because you're almost home, perhaps because you've been climbing all day. After reaching the top, pedal 7 more miles and you're back to Highway 3, which features a long, luscious descent back into Weaverville.

From here you can look back at the Trinity Alps looming impossibly high in the distance and think about how far you've gone, about all the miles of climbing you've hammered into your muscles. From Weaverville's valley the distant mountains look murderous, hard-core. But in the afterglow of the ride, all pain is forgotten and anything seems possible. Tuck that feeling away in some corner of your mind and don't let go of it. A time will inevitably come when you'll need to rely on the glory of the past to pull you through the pain of the present. Because

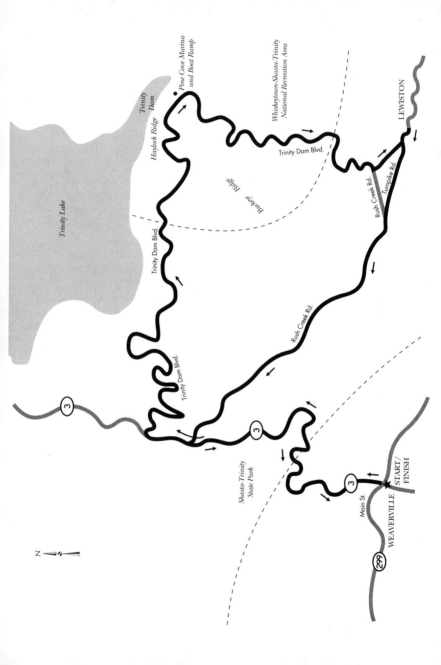

Trinity Lake

Trinity Dam

Haylock Ridge

Pine Cove Marina
and Boat Ramp

Whiskeytown-Shasta-Trinity
National Recreation Area

Trinity Dam Blvd.

Buckeye Ridge

LEWISTON

Trinity Dam Blvd.

Rush Creek Rd.

Turnpike Rd.

Rush Creek Rd.

3

Shasta-Trinity
State Park

3

Trinity Dam Blvd.

3

Main St.

299

WEAVERVILLE

START/
FINISH

N

there will always be another challenge. There will always be a higher mountain to climb.

The Basics

Start: Intersection of Hwy. 299 and Hwy. 3 in downtown Weaverville.
Length: 44.8 miles.
Terrain: Mountain roads, many extended climbs, few flat sections; narrow roads with little traffic, but watch for occasional logging trucks.
Food: There's a good health food store right on Main Street in Weaverville where you can stock up on food for the ride. Upon departing Weaverville, you'll find no opportunities for food until Lewiston (mile 28), where the Lewiston Market has a limited selection. Back in Weaverville there are plenty of postride restaurants.
For more information: The owner of the Old Lewiston Inn has mapped out bike routes in the area for his B&B guests. Contact Connor Nixon, Deadwood Rd. Historic Area, P.O. Box 688, Lewiston, CA 96052; (800) 286–4441. Ellison's Bicycle Shop, 105 Weaver St., Weaverville, CA 96093; (530) 623–3377. Most cyclists in the area are mountain bikers. Bring your mountain bike, too, if you can. There are endless miles of fire roads and single-track trails.

Miles & Directions

- 0.0 Take Hwy. 3 toward Trinity from Main St. (Hwy. 299) in downtown Weaverville; begin climbing out of town. On this section of Hwy. 3 be sure to watch for logging trucks.
- 2.8 Summit.
- 4.2 Enter Shasta-Trinity State Park.
- 8.1 Right onto Trinity Dam Blvd.; begin climbing.

- 10.5 Summit at intersection of Haylock Ridge (to the left) and Buckeye Ridge (to the right). Continue straight.
- 12.9 Enter Whiskeytown-Shasta-Trinity National Recreation Area.
- 13.4 Begin climbing again!
- 14.7 Summit.
- 16.7 Trinity Vista Overlook; begin descent.
- 19.2 Trinity Dam Vista.
- 22.9 Pass Pine Cove Marina and Boat Ramp.
- 25.0 Copper Gulch Campground; begin another climb.
- 25.9 Summit.
- 27.2 Leave Whiskeytown-Shasta-Trinity National Recreation Area.
- 27.8 Straight past Rush Creek Rd. and the sign TO WEAVERVILLE.
- 27.9 Right onto Deadwood Rd.
- 28.0 Lewiston.
- 28.8 Right onto Turnpike Rd. over old bridge.
- 29.0 Left onto Rush Creek Rd.; begin climbing.
- 30.0 Summit.
- 37.6 Left onto Hwy. 3 to Weaverville. Watch for logging trucks on this section or road.
- 43.4 Weaverville city limits.
- 44.8 Ride ends at Main St. in Weaverville.

North San Francisco Bay Area

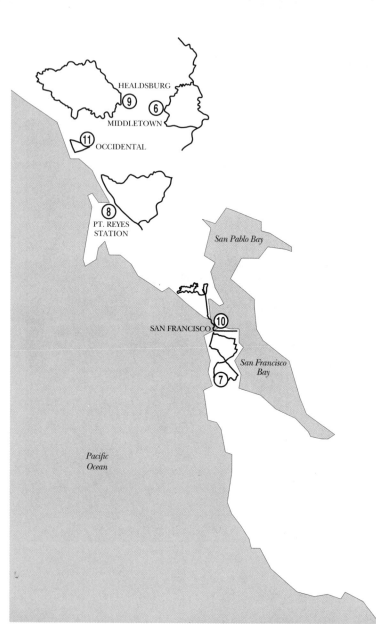

HEALDSBURG

⑨

⑥

MIDDLETOWN

⑪ OCCIDENTAL

⑧

PT. REYES
STATION

San Pablo Bay

SAN FRANCISCO ⑩

San Francisco
Bay

⑦

Pacific
Ocean

North San Francisco Bay Area

6

Harbin Hot Springs Challenge

*Harbin Hot Springs—Middletown—Petrified Forest—
Calistoga—Harbin Hot Springs*

> *Riding a bike with no shirt on is very fun. Especially in
> the rain. Makes you ride faster, too.*
> —Greta Snyder, *Mudflap*

If you've ever felt weighed down by the clothes on your back,
it's time to shed all superfluous coverings and head for Harbin
Hot Springs, a clothing-optional, 1,200-acre resort resting se-
dately in the hills of California's Lake County, just two hours
northeast of San Francisco. No California experience is truly
complete without a trip to Harbin, which is run by the Heart
Consciousness Church, a New Age group advocating holistic
health and spiritual renewal. And no bike book is complete
without a tour of the area's surrounding backroads, which have
the power to bring even the most ardent heathens closer to
God. This land is nothing short of divine.

To understand how cool the Harbin Hot Springs resort is, try
the following exercise. Dream up your perfect day of cycling
and then compare it with this:

A warm day of riding on secluded roads. Nary a car nor a cyclist in sight. Killer climbs and unsurpassed hilltop views. Un-
traveled pavement spiraling endlessly downward. Weary limbs
and endorphin highs at ride's end. And then: soft, natural spring

pools of varying temperatures to soak in. A sauna. A masseuse. Sunbathing on redwood decks. A huge vegetarian meal prepared for you. A free movie. A night of peaceful sleep among the redwoods—beside a babbling brook or in a cozy cabin.

This is not a dream. You have not gone to biker heaven; you've gone to Harbin. The Harbin Hot Springs Challenge is not just a ride. And you don't do it in one day. It's more like a life experience—with some awesome cycling thrown in to make it all the better. The good folks at Harbin have made camping easy and desirable with gorgeous wooded surroundings and redwood decks built especially for pitching your tent. (Should you have to get dirty when you camp? Perish the thought!) So make a weekend out of this ride—or longer, if you can manage it. If you plan to camp or park at Harbin, expect to pay something. You can be a day visitor until 9:00 P.M., camp, or have a room with a bath. Reservations are suggested.

While topless or naked cycling certainly wouldn't turn many heads on Harbin's property, clothing is highly recommended for the outlying country roads that this ride traverses. Also recommended is a road bike with wide, durable tires—such as Continental touring tires—or a mountain bike or good hybrid. The 3-mile climb up Western Mine Road turns from pavement to dirt fire road after the first mile. This is the only dirt road on the entire ride, but the bumpy road does demand some attention to equipment. There's also a greater potential for flatting, so make doubly sure you've got a spare tube as well as a patch kit.

The steep and tiring Western Mine climb begins after only 6.7 miles of cycling. The road turns to dirt at mile 7.7 and becomes paved again at the summit (mile 9.9). After all the jostling and sweating to get to the top, the smooth, picturesque, and never-ending descent can only be described as godlike. For the next 20 miles, the route is completely and utterly rural. You'll pass few homes and even fewer cars on the ride. And if you do feel the urge to ride naked, these nearly deserted roads are probably the best upon which to do it.

Cyclists continue to be treated to this noble countryside until they reach Petrified Forest Road, which involves a more trafficky climb and finally leads to the Petrified Forest at mile 30.5. Get off your bike and take a look around. After you've had your fill, it's back to Petrified Forest Road for 4 miles until hitting Highway 128 and, 1 mile later, the less crowded Highway 29.

The ride gets even more touristy here as you cycle into Calistoga, land of commercialized hot springs and spas. Land of restaurants and amenities, cute shops, and a great bike shop, Palisades Mountain Sport. It's a great place to stop, but after a hard day of riding, you'll be glad you're staying on Harbin's tranquil, laid-back land.

From Calistoga it's a straight shot back to Middletown on Highway 29. Be prepared for 2,000 feet of climbing on the slopes Mt. St. Helena to Robert Louis Stevenson State Park. This is a narrow, winding road with traffic, especially on the weekends. Once back in Middletown, you're 5 miles away from a luxurious soak and a huge, holistic feast at Harbin.

The Basics

Start: Harbin Hot Springs campground. From Hwy. 101 in Geyserville, take Rte. 128 east to Calistoga, then Rte. 29 north to Middletown. Turn left at the stoplight, then right at Barnes Rd. Four miles to Harbin Springs Rd., which leads to Harbin Hot Springs.

Length: 57.9 miles.

Terrain: Extended climbing and lengthy descents. Some rough roads, including 1 mile of dirt fire road. Mostly rural roads, with a few high-traffic areas.

Food: At Harbin Hot Springs, in addition to the restaurant, which serves breakfast (order the pancake) and dinner, there are two coffee cafes and a general store. An all-purpose convenience store and a health food store are located in Middletown, at 4.2 miles. No more food options until Calistoga, at 35.3 miles.

For more information: Harbin Hot Springs, P.O. Box 782, Middletown, CA 95461; (707) 987–2477. Palisades Mountain Sport, 1330 B Gerrard St., Calistoga, CA 94515; (707) 942–9687.

Miles & Directions

- 0.0   Harbin Hot Springs camping area, Harbin Springs Rd.
- 2.8   Veer right onto Big Canyon Rd. Big Canyon becomes Barnes Rd.
- 4.2   Left onto Main St. into Middletown
- 4.4   Right onto Rte. 29.
- 6.7   Right onto Western Mine Rd.
- 7.7   Road turns to dirt.
- 9.9   Summit. Road becomes Ida Clayton Rd. and turns back to pavement. *Caution!* Steep, winding descent on one-lane road.
- 10.9   Trout farm.
- 18.1   Left on Rte. 29 (unmarked).
- 18.3   Right onto Franz Valley Rd.
- 19.2   Stay to the right and continue on Franz Valley Rd.
- 22.8   Left onto Franz Valley School Rd.
- 25.4   Enter Napa County.
- 27.3   Road ends at Petrified Forest Rd.; turn right.
- 30.5   Petrified Forest, turnaround point. Turn left back onto Petrified Forest Rd.
- 34.4   Right onto Rte. 128.
- 35.3   Left onto Rte. 29 into Calistoga.
- 52.3   Left onto Main St. in Middletown
- 52.5   Right onto Barnes Rd.
- 55.1   Left onto Harbin Springs Rd.
- 57.9   Ride ends at Harbin Hot Springs camping area.

7

San Francisco to Mt. San Bruno Urban Cruise

*Golden Gate Park—Great Highway—the Sunset—
Daly City—Mt. San Bruno State Park—the Mission—
the Castro—Golden Gate Park*

> *Forget the damned motor car and build cities for lovers
> and friends.*
>
> —Lewis Mumford, *My Work and Days*

There are cyclists out there who spend their entire lives seeking nirvana in the ultimate backroad. Tirelessly, doggedly, idealistically, they search for that transcendent stretch of tarmac that will elevate their cycling from a recreational outlet to a spiritual experience.

If you've been riding long enough, you've no doubt felt that place where body, soul, and bicycle come together for a brief moment of unworldly ecstasy. And it sends you. And you want more. A more beautiful road. A higher peak. A more peaceful portion of pavement.

Funny thing is, the path to enlightenment is quite often the obvious path, the one that's been there all along. Such is the joy of the urban ride: the blurred colors and smells of city life, the cacophony of the street sounds buzzing in your ears, the self-sufficiency of using your bike for transportation and exploration—not just for recreation.

This is the beauty of the San Francisco to Mt. San Bruno Urban Cruise. The subtleties of San Francisco living, of the reality of urban existence, are what this ride is all about. The ride starts in Golden Gate Park. As you begin your trek at the brilliant green lawn of the bright white, fairy-tale-like building that houses the plant conservatory, the muted colors of the city are washed away and replaced by blue skies, green grass, and pink tulips.

But this brilliant departure from reality is short-lived. After 5 miles of riding, the relative peace of the park and the paradisiacal ocean views from the Great Highway are replaced by car doors flinging open, booming bass droning from stereos, and the pungent emissions of stagnant garbage, heavy exhaust, and roasted coffee. Tiny neighborhoods and microcosmic communities dot your path as you head up Mission Street toward the outskirts of town, with Mt. San Bruno drawing nearer—and your impending climb seeming all the bigger.

The mountain trudge begins at mile 13.5 and doesn't let up until you summit Mt. San Bruno at mile 16.7. *California Bicyclist's* former Associate Editor Barbara Hanscome describes the climb, which is the site of a traditional New Year's Day hillclimb race, as "guaranteeing anaerobic agony for any cyclist who dares to climb it."

Whatever agony you may experience, the view from the top is well worth flexing your quads over. If it's not storming, freezing, or blowing you over up there, stop long enough to check out the view. Turn one way and you'll see downtown San Francisco, the Bay Bridge, and the East Bay stretching out into the distance. Walk to the other side and survey the peninsula's sprawling suburbs, the majestic Golden Gate Bridge, and the distant Pacific Ocean. From your peaceful mountaintop vista, the urban sprawl that you and your bike were recently battling seems sedated and calmed—almost still. The chaos of a million personal dramas are being played out below you, yet for this one moment everything is serene, virtually soundless except for the whipping wind.

Get the most out of your descent as you snake back into the city, because the return route includes one more steep, punchy climb at mile 25, as you tackle an obligatory short but steep San Francisco hill on Dolores Street.

Your final 3 miles of riding traverse through two of San Francisco's most interesting neighborhoods: the Mission and the Castro. If you haven't spend much time in San Francisco, you'll definitely want some out-of-the-saddle exploring time in at least one of these areas. And if you've worked up an appetite, take a right onto Dolores Street into the heart of the Mission for a monster burrito like you won't find anywhere else.

From here it's an easy ride back to Golden Gate Park and the conservatory, where you can join other cyclists and random fun lovers sprawled out on the abnormally bright green lawn. You've earned a right to dwell in the denial of the park's man-made perfection for a while, because you've seen reality. And you know that, in its own way, it's even better.

The Basics

Start: Golden Gate Park Conservatory. Enter the park at Stanyan St., and the conservatory is the large white building about 0.3 mile in on the main road, John F. Kennedy Dr.
Length: 28.1 miles.
Terrain: Abrupt, short but steep hills in San Francisco. One major climb up Mt. San Bruno. Potholes, ever-changing road construction sites, and narrow streets in the city.
Food: No real restaurants or stores in the park. Visit nearby Haight Street for stores where you can stock up on ride food or grab a slice of pizza or a burrito. Better yet, take a quick detour into the Mission at Mission Dolores Park (mile 25.2) and visit La Cumbre (515 Valencia) or one of the many other *taquerias* for the best burritos the city has to offer.
For more information: San Francisco Convention and Visitors' Bureau, 201 3rd St., Suite 900, San Francisco, CA 94103; (415) 391–2000. American Cyclery Since 1941, 510 Frederick St., San Francisco, CA 94117; (415) 664–4545.

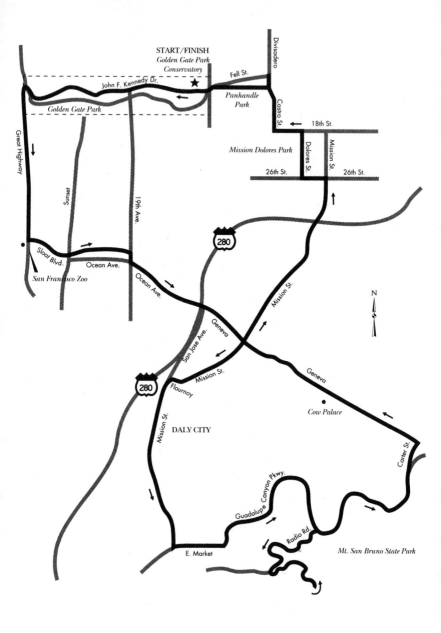

Miles & Directions

- 0.0   From Golden Gate Park Conservatory, turn right onto John F. Kennedy Dr.
- 2.0   Stay on the main road as you pass the unmarked road around the lake to your left.
- 2.1   Buffalo field
- 2.7   Turn right, still on John F. Kennedy Dr.
- 3.1   Pacific Ocean! Turn left onto Great Highway.
- 5.6   Turn left onto Sloat Blvd.
- 5.7   San Francisco Zoo.
- 7.4   Turn right onto 19th Ave.
- 7.5   Turn left onto Ocean Ave.
- 9.1   Veer right. Ocean Ave. ends; Geneva begins.
- 9.3   Cross over Hwy. 280.
- 9.8   Turn right onto Mission St.
- 11.1   Turn right onto Flournoy. Flournoy is a small street that comes in when Mission becomes one-way.
- 11.2   Turn left onto San Jose Ave. Becomes Mission again. Entering Daly City.
- 12.5   Turn left onto E. Market.
- 13.5   E. Market becomes Guadalupe Canyon Pkwy. Pass sign ENTERING MT. SAN BRUNO STATE PARK. Begin climb.
- 14.8   Turn left at Mt. San Bruno State Park entrance. Take immediate right past ranger station onto Summit Rd. (also known as Tower Rd. or Radio Rd., but don't worry about names—there's not even a sign for it).
- 15.0   Ride under overpass.
- 16.7   Summit at radio towers. Turnaround point.
- 18.3   Turn left at ranger station.
- 18.4   Turn left three times in quick succession to head east on Guadalupe Canyon Pkwy.
- 19.6   Turn left onto Carter St.
- 19.9   Cow Palace.
- 20.3   Turn left onto Geneva.
- 21.4   Turn right onto Mission St.

- 22.7   Ride over freeway overpass; stay on Mission St.
- 24.1   Turn left onto 26th St.
- 24.5   Turn right onto Dolores St.
- 25.2   Mission Dolores Park.
- 25.4   Turn left onto 18th St.
- 25.9   Turn right onto Castro St.
- 26.6   Castro St. becomes Divisadero.
- 26.8   Left onto Fell St.
- 27.1   Panhandle Park parallel to Fell St. Get on bike path to avoid dog-eat-dog traffic scene.
- 27.8   Panhandle ends. Enter Golden Gate Park.
- 28.1   Ride ends at conservatory.

8

Cheese Company Cruise

Marin French Cheese Company—Marshall—Point Reyes Station—Marin French Cheese Company

> *Savor the accidental, perfect beauty of life in whatever small portions are dished out to you. And never question why you ride. Question only why you don't ride more.*
> —Mike Ferrentino, *California Bicyclist*

You know you're a real bicyclist when you actually start liking the smell of cow dung. It happens on pastoral roads as you're cycling past dumb, lovable cows that stare you down with their deep black eyes. And you're riding. And the sky is blue and the grass is green and the gentle breeze carries with it the smell of—cow dung. And for the first time ever, you find the odor wonderful and you breathe it in deeply and you ride and you're oh-so-happy just to be alive.

The Cheese Company Cruise is the kind of ride that has this potential. If you've never loved cows or the smell of their relievings, take this ride and then see how you feel. Its idyllic setting is made all the more beautiful precisely because you smell cows and ride past big sturdy barns. And when you do, you can almost feel the dignity and understand the truth behind the simple, hardworking lifestyle of the farmers who live there.

The ride begins at the Marin French Cheese Company, located on the Point Reyes–Petaluma Road between Novato and Petaluma. This is a popular bike ride for local cyclists, and you'll probably run into some of them relaxing on the cheese company's lawn while they recover or take a break from riding.

With its luscious cheeses and meticulously manicured property, the Marin French Cheese Company is the most commercialized spot on the entire bike route. Once you step into your pedals and turn onto Hicks Valley Road, you roll into a different world.

The first 10 miles provide fast and easy riding on intensely rural roads. Your whirring wheels and rhythmic breathing are the only audible sounds, and as you settle into this trancelike quiet, it's almost impossible to believe that you're only 40 miles away from the urban sprawl of San Francisco and its surrounding areas.

After exactly 10 miles you reach what's known by cyclists as the Marshall Wall. This 2-mile climb is an unrelenting pull with at least two false summits that laugh in your face as they reveal yet another hill for your downtrodden legs to tackle. Still, the name is more intimidating than the actual climb. And once you get to the top, the views of Point Reyes and Tomales Bay are absolutely euphoric. Then again, maybe it's just those endorphins that are coursing through your body.

The backside of the Marshall Wall is much steeper and makes for a great descent that you'll be thankful not to have to return on. Down in the tiny town of Marshall, you'll find rickety oyster bars and a few random stores perched on the edge of Tomales Bay. Following the Shoreline Highway, you'll get a rollercoaster ride of whoop-di-do pavement that's often made easier by benevolent tailwinds. After nearly 7 miles of this fun, you'll experience a few longer climbs before dropping down into the tiny burg of Point Reyes Station, a holistic little town with lots of charm and plenty of healthy food—so fuel up for your home stretch back to the cheese company.

You get even more sweet cows, rural scenery, and peaceful country-road stuff on the way back. And, of course, as fate would have it, there's another major climb less than 4 miles from the end of the ride. This final push begins just past the Nicasio Reservoir and heads upward on a fairly busy road back to the cheese company, where you can chill out and mooch free samples of cheese. Proper etiquette dictates that you do eventually buy something, but don't feel shy about sampling the goods. Even in your sweaty, dirty bike clothes, sporting your freshly plastered helmet-head, you won't be shunned—this is biking territory, and the folks are used to our kind here.

The Basics

Start: Marin French Cheese Company, Point Reyes–Petaluma Rd. Take Hwy. 101 to downtown Novato. From there take Novato Blvd. east until it intersects with Point Reyes–Petaluma Rd.
Length: 34.5 miles.
Terrain: Two major climbs; lots of rolling hills on smooth, quiet roads.
Food: The cheese company has—you guessed it—lots of cheese and cheese-related snacks, as well as chips, sodas, and delicious fruit. If you like raw oysters, stop in Marshall at one of the bayside oyster bars. Otherwise, you can stock up on snacks in Point Reyes Station, where there are several cafes and a great grocery store situated right on the main road.
For more information: Petaluma Visitors Program, 799 Baywood Dr., Suite 1, Petaluma, CA 94954; (707) 762–2785. Bikadelic Bikestore and Espresso Cafe, 8 Bolinas Rd., Fairfax, CA 94930; (415) 460–9792.

Miles & Directions

- 0.0 From the cheese company, turn left onto Point Reyes–Petaluma Rd.
- 0.9 Left onto Hicks Valley/Wilson Hill Rd. to Marshall.
- 3.6 Left on Marshall–Petaluma Rd.
- 10.0 S/2 Aberdeen Angus Cattle Ranch. Begin climb up Marshall Wall!
- 12.0 Summit.
- 14.6 Marshall. Left onto Shoreline Hwy.

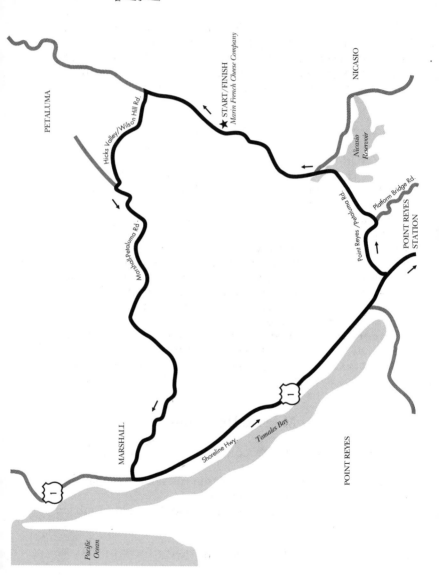

N

PETALUMA

Hicks Valley/Wilson Hill Rd.

★ START/FINISH
Marin French Cheese Company

NICASIO

Nicasio Reservoir

Point Reyes/Petaluma Rd.

Platform Bridge Rd.

POINT REYES STATION

Marshall/Petaluma Rd.

MARSHALL

Shoreline Hwy.

Tomales Bay

POINT REYES

Pacific Ocean

- 23.7 Veer right, staying on Hwy. 1 (formerly Shoreline Hwy.) into Point Reyes Station.
- 24.0 Point Reyes Station. Turnaround point. After sightseeing, ride back up the hill on Hwy. 1.
- 24.2 Veer right onto Point Reyes–Petaluma Rd.
- 28.1 Left at T intersection onto Platform Bridge Rd.
- 28.9 Nicasio Reservoir.
- 31.1 Begin climb.
- 32.6 Summit.
- 34.5 Ride ends at Marin French Cheese Company.

9

Skaggs Springs Classic

Healdsburg—Dry Creek—Lake Sonoma—
Skaggs Springs—Cazadero—Monte Rio—
Guerneville—Rio Nido—Healdsburg

Elected Silence, sing to me/And beat upon my whorled
ear,/Pipe me to pastures still and be/The music that I
care to hear.
—Gerard Manley Hopkins, "The Habit of Perfection"

Think of Sonoma County and you're likely to envision miles of electric green hills with ribbons of gnarled vines woven into their undulations. Sonoma, the less touristy sister county to the famed Napa, spreads over rich and varied countryside, rising to stony gray peaks and dropping into fertile green valleys, stretching from the sun-drenched Russian River to the rocky shores of the Pacific Ocean. And while stately wineries and gently rolling country roads are Sonoma's main attractions, most people don't even realize how much more it has to offer. This tiny corner of the world is so deliciously fascinating that it seems almost imaginary. Could real life possibly be this fantastical?

Your ride begins in downtown Healdsburg, a wine-country community where you'll probably encounter more locals than tourists. The town's hub of activity centers on a redwood-lined town square that's filled with cafes and nouvelle-cuisine restaurants. As you ride out of town on Healdsburg Avenue, you'll pass the planned communities and schools of the Healdsburg residents before plunging into the countryside in all its splendor. And when you cross under Highway 101 on your bike, you make a symbolic gesture to the natural world: Nature promises you a gateway to some of its best-kept secrets. In return, you promise to leave the material worries of cars and office cubicles on the other side of that freeway.

The serpentine curves of Dry Creek Road provide an up-close communion with meticulously tended vineyards that roll along a brilliant green carpet. In the distance, hills swallowed by swarms of trees provide a foreshadowing of things to come. As the road gets narrower and traffic thins out, you leave the vineyards behind and forge onward to Lake Sonoma, where tourists, campers, and anglers alike come to frolic on the man-made (but quite lovely) lake.

From here a mega-climb awaits. It's the kind of ascent that, like a well-decorated fish story, will be elevated to legendary status just hours after you conquer it. But before that happens, you'll have to get through it. Do not succumb to the trickery of this climb. With its ridges that look so much like summits, it lures you into a false confidence, only to crush you mercilessly by revealing yet another uphill grade at the exact moment you thought you were done. But from the top, some 16 miles later, all the lung-burning, heart-pounding agony pays off. As you wipe the salt out of your eyes, you'll see hawks gliding low overhead and cows lolling in the clearing. The cold air and silent pasturelands make the warm valley vineyards, hidden in the folds of far-below hills, seem worlds away. For this moment, chances are mighty good that you and your cycling partners will have the world to yourselves, and that you will have forgotten all about overcrowded cities and traffic jams. Chances are, you will have kept your pact with Nature.

The ecstasy of the summit is followed by miles of easy riding through unadulterated countryside and lush forests. The closer you get to the Pacific Ocean, the damper, darker, and mossier your surroundings become. But this ride is a study in contrasts, and as you veer away from the nearing ocean, the trees change dramatically, until you are once again amid idyllic pastureland, feeling like some character in a Wordsworth poem. You are alone as ever, except for cows lounging silently at the sides of the road and wandering aimlessly through deserted barns. Fences are unnecessary, for there is no reason to flee this beautiful place. Even the cows understand this.

The inevitable swooshing descent finally comes as the road spirals downward to Cazadero. After more than 50 miles of townless roads and nothing but the sounds of a rushing creek or a tree rustling in the breeze, you have once again reached civilization. Even so, except for a heavily trafficked stint on Highway 116, the roads, especially Austin Creek Road, are peaceful, gently nudging your tired limbs back to Healdsburg. And if the fertile soil and healthy souls of Healdsburg, Guerneville, and the Russian River are what civilization is all about, then, by God, it's not half-bad.

The Basics

Start: Intersection of Healdsburg Ave. and Matheson St. in downtown Healdsburg, north of Santa Rosa off Hwy. 101.
Length: 100.7 miles.
Terrain: Extended climbing, steeply graded ascents, rolling hills, some rough roads. Be in good shape!
Food: There are lots of cafes and restaurants in Healdsburg at the ride start/finish. Stock up on on-the-ride munchies in town, because you won't see another store until you reach Cazadero at mile 68.4. From then on there are plenty of markets, restaurants, and phones if you need to bail.
For more information: Lake Sonoma Recreation Area, 3333 Skaggs Springs Rd., Geyserville, CA 95441; (707) 433–9483. Dave's Bike Sport, 353 College Ave., Santa Rosa, CA 95401; (707) 528–3283. The Skaggs Springs loop forms the second half of the Terrible Two, a classic double century held in Sonoma County each June. For Terrible Two information, call (707) 823–9807.

Miles & Directions

- 0.0 Intersection of Healdsburg Ave. and Matheson St. in downtown Healdsburg. Head north on Healdsburg Ave. past the town square.
- 0.7 Road curves past a 7-Eleven; continue straight on Healdsburg Ave.
- 1.1 Left onto Dry Creek Rd.
- 1.4 Cross underneath Hwy. 101. Continue straight on Dry Creek Rd.
- 4.5 Dry Creek.
- 5.5 Dry Creek Rd. narrows.
- 11.9 Lake Sonoma Visitor Center and Fish Hatchery. Continue straight into the park.
- 12.2 Begin climbing.
- 13.7 Left on Stewarts Point/Skaggs Springs Rd. Follow signs TO OVERLOOK and TO MARINA.
- 14.2 Turn right for a quick side trip to Lake Sonoma Overlook; steep uphill grade.
- 14.7 Lake Sonoma Overlook.
- 15.1 Turn right back onto Stewarts Point/Skaggs Springs Rd.; continue climbing.
- 16.0 Short climbing reprieve.
- 17.4 Begin climbing again.
- 22.0 Summit.
- 26.2 Road becomes narrower and gravelly; begin another climb.
- 28.3 Summit.
- 41.0 Pass YMCA camp.
- 43.3 Pass Annapolis Rd. and old metal bridge; continue straight.
- 43.9 Cross one-lane bridge.
- 44.1 Begin climbing.
- 45.5 Summit. Left onto Tin Barn Rd.
- 51.4 Left onto King Ridge Rd. Follow sign TO CAZADERO.
- 60.0 Long descent begins; rough road.

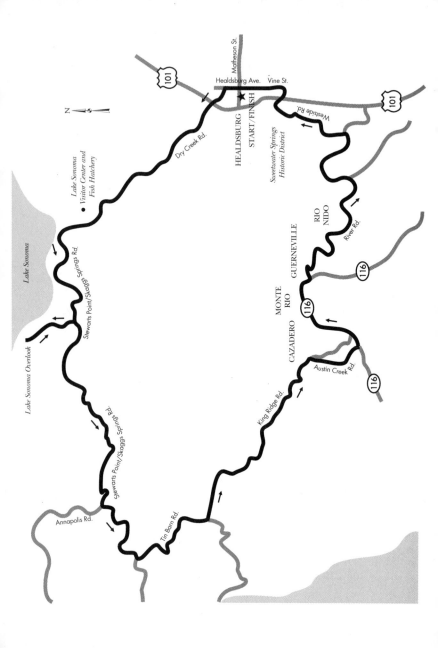

- 67.8 Road diverges. Continue straight on main road.
- 68.1 Stop sign. Continue straight, following Cazadero Hwy.
- 68.4 Cazadero.
- 68.6 Veer onto Austin Creek Rd.
- 71.6 Austin Creek Rd. crosses Old Cazadero Hwy. Continue straight.
- 75.3 Left onto Hwy. 116 (River Rd.) to Monte Rio.
- 77.7 Monte Rio.
- 78.0 Stop sign; continue straight on River Rd.
- 82.2 Guerneville.
- 82.3 Stop sign; continue straight on River Rd.
- 83.9 Rio Nido.
- 85.2 Pass Korbel Winery.
- 87.7 Left onto Westside Rd.
- 90.7 Westside Rd. intersects with road to Santa Rosa; continue straight.
- 94.4 Pass Sweetwater Springs Historic District.
- 99.6 Pass W. Dry Creek Rd.; continue straight.
- 100.3 Cross under Hwy. 101; continue straight.
- 100.4 Healdsburg city limits.
- 100.5 Left onto Vine St.
- 100.7 Ride ends at intersection of Healdsburg Ave. and Matheson St.

10

Headlands Loop Cruise

Fort Mason—Marina Green—
San Francisco Presidio—Golden Gate Bridge—
Marin Headlands—Fort Mason

East is East and West is San Francisco, according to Cal-
ifornians. Californians are a race of people; they are not
merely inhabitants of a state. They are the Southerners of
the West.
　　　　　　　　　—William Sydney Porter, *A Municipal Report*

Bicycling in San Francisco is often like riding in the muddy gray
shades of a black-and-white television screen. The wind off the
Pacific whips tears from your eyes, and fog hangs eerily over the
city, casting a gray shadow on even the brightest of colors. But
hop on your bike and pedal just a few miles over the Golden
Gate Bridge and your gray scale is magically transformed into
the Technicolor, sun-baked hues of Marin. It's at this moment—as the bridge's immense, brick-colored towers escort you
away from the city—that you'll be reminded of just how great it
is to be riding in the diverse state of California. As you reach the
edge of the bridge, the Coastal Mountain Range unfolds gener-
ously into the lapping shores of the ocean. The fog has disap-
peared. The hills are innocent of development. You are
pedaling into another perfect day in Marin County. It's like
being transported to another land, and the feeling is undeni-

ably dramatic—as magical as the famed tornado that carried Dorothy and Toto from Kansas to Oz.

While San Francisco is not always gray and Marin is not always blue, this is the general state of affairs—at least during the summer months. On any given weekend you'll see droves of cyclists making their mass exodus to Marin via that symbolic bridge of long departures and triumphant returns, the Golden Gate.

The Headlands Loop Cruise begins at Fort Mason Center, located on the very edge of San Francisco's Marina Green. This rectangular park stretches along the shores of the San Francisco Bay, from Fort Mason to the Presidio Army Base.

The Presidio is currently embroiled in the intricate legal process of transforming from army base to state park. From the verdant lawn of the Marina Green, you are dropped into an army base in the processes of abandonment. The stiff wind races through empty, boarded-up barracks lining Mason Street, giving it the impression of a military ghost town. Some troops are still on base, however, and you can see them meandering around in camouflage, blending right in with the tall, leafy eucalyptus trees that squeak creepily in the breeze. As you roll past the colorful pet cemetery and up the snaky Lincoln Boulevard, a string of increasingly beautiful vistas of the bay flaunt their conspicuous beauty. The Golden Gate Bridge, with its formidable red towers claiming much of the foreground, stands enmeshed amid the natural beauty of the sailboat-dotted bay, the immense Pacific Ocean, and Marin's soft hills.

Across the bridge your route dives into the hills of the Marin Headlands Golden Gate National Recreation Area and begins climbing. Conzelman Road twists above the Pacific Ocean, and before long you are high above the bridge and city—and whatever stresses you may have felt are back on the other side of the bay. The climb is steep but relatively short, and the views of the ocean, the bay, the bridge, and the fair city of San Francisco far exceed the pain-and-sweat factor.

From the top you'll be treated to a swirling, drop-off-the-

START/FINISH

Fort Mason

Laguna St.

Marina St.

Marina Green

Mason St.

pet cemetery

Cowles St.

Crissy Field Ave.

Crissy Field

Lincoln Blvd.

Fort Point

San Francisco Bay

Alcatraz Island

N

Golden Gate Bridge

101

Alexander Ave.

Marin County

Marin Headlands

Conzelman Rd.

Bunker Rd.

Bunker Rd.

Conzelman Rd.

Pt. Bonita

Lincoln Blvd.

Presidio

101

face-of-the-earth downhill that leads to the valley floor of the Headlands, as well as to the beach. Go slower than you think you need to. As you first drop down the other side, there's a steep hairpin turn just waiting to cause problems for inattentive cyclists. From the bottom of the hill, the options abound for cyclists wishing to explore the Headlands. Turn left for a short jaunt out to the Point Bonita Lighthouse. Here you can't miss the old Nike Missile Site. Where we once had missiles targeted on Russian cities, there is now only a ghost town. To check out the beach, make another left just past the visitor center. For those in need of accommodations, there is a youth hostel with bunk beds for only $12.00 a night.

As Bunker Road begins its climb back to Conzelman, you'll understand why so many cyclists use these roads for training: hills. In fact, this is probably one of the toughest cruises listed in this book. No sooner have you patted yourself on the back for conquering Conzelman than you're back at it again. But one of the most charming aspects of this ride (depending on your mindset) is that it's short. When Bunker hits Conzelman, you're home free. It's basically downhill all the way back to the city, where you'll probably be needing that windbreaker you brought along.

The Basics

Start: Fort Mason Center, at Laguna St. and Marina St. in San Francisco.
Length: 16.8 miles.
Terrain: Hilly roads; high traffic on weekends.
Food: Safeway supermarket at ride start; get snacks there, because there ain't no snack bars in the Headlands.
For more information: American Youth Hostels, 312 Mason St., San Francisco, CA 94102; (415) 788–5604. City Cycle, 3001 Steiner St., San Francisco, CA 94123; (415) 346–2242.

Miles & Directions

- 0.0 From Fort Mason Center, corner of Laguna St. and Marina St., head west to Golden Gate Bridge.
- 0.5 Enter Presidio; continue straight, following Mason St.
- 1.9 Left on Crissy Field Ave. at stop sign.
- 2.0 Right on Cowles St., just past pet cemetery.
- 2.2 Right on Lincoln Blvd.
- 2.6 Veer right onto bike path at Fort Point.
- 2.9 Follow sign directing you to the Golden Gate Bridge's left (west-side) bikeway/sidewalk on weekends and holidays, and to the right (east-side) bikeway/sidewalk on weekdays. (This route's mileage is calculated from the right side of the bridge, thus making it approximately 1 mile longer.)
- 4.1 Marin County line.
- 4.9 Cross Alexander Ave. and turn left, heading under subway.
- 5.2 Veer right toward Marin Headlands; begin climbing on Conzelman Rd.
- 6.2 Veer left, continuing upward on Conzelman Rd.
- 7.0 Summit.
- 7.1 Begin steep descent down Conzelman (one-way traffic, down only).
- 8.2 After the cattle guard, you make a hairpin right turn on Conzelman.
- 10.3 Right onto Bunker Rd.; begin climb.
- 11.6 Summit; left onto Conzelman.
- 12.6 Left onto service road, under subway; cross Alexander to Golden Gate Bridge bikeway.
- 13.2 Golden Gate Bridge.
- 14.9 Follow bike path back to Lincoln Blvd.
- 15.2 Left onto Lincoln Blvd.
- 15.6 Left onto Cowles.
- 15.8 Left onto Crissy Field Ave.
- 15.9 Right onto Mason.
- 16.3 Mason becomes Marina St.
- 16.8 Ride ends at Fort Mason Center.

11

Occidental Cruise

*Occidental—Coleman Valley—The Coast—
The Russian River—Occidental*

> *The ratio of cars in the front yard to populace certainly
> has to exceed 2:1, inspiring those of us with shaved legs
> and Lycra to keep up a good pace through town.*
> —Rob Schott

The town of Occidental is a tiny redwood getaway on the western edge of Sonoma County, between Santa Rosa and the ocean. Founded as a railhead for the lumber industry, Occidental now thrives on retirees, tourists, and its many restaurants. Occidental also happens to be one of the most charming towns in California.

The Occidental Cruise is another redwoods-to-the-sea ride, really the best type of ride in this part of the country because of the remarkable contrasts. Beginning in the lush, ferny, dimly lit world of the Bohemian Highway, the route traverses open meadows to reach a spectacular aerial view of the Pacific Ocean. Then after 10 miles of brightly lit seascape on Highway 1, the cruise returns to the redwoods on the stair-stepped dirt of Willow Creek Road.

The start is at Gianni Cyclery, the smallest, coolest bike shop you're likely to visit. If you feel real touristy, you can purchase some of the shop's trademark hot sauce or maybe a cycling cap. Gianni is the sponsor of the infamous Ring of

Fire mountain bike race and celebration, held around Occidental in late September.

Leaving Occidental, the Occidental Cruise climbs out of the Bohemian Valley on Coleman Valley Road. Watch for blackberries along this stretch of road from mid-summer onward. Also on this stretch is the old Coleman Valley School, one of the oldest schoolhouses in California (1864), which stands to the left of the road. The terrain on Coleman is rolling and opens into meadows that lead through a series of sheep and goat farms reminiscent of Ireland and finally to the abrupt 1,000-foot descent of Irish Hill to Highway 1.

Cyclists should take care on Highway 1 because of tourist traffic, especially on weekends. Water can be found at Pomo Creek. Interesting side trips include Shell Beach, where there are hiking trails, and Goat Rock. If you have a need for espresso, a spin up to Jenner is 3 or 4 miles. The Sizzling Tandoor at the base of Willow Creek Road is known for its great Indian food.

Willow Creek presents quite a contrast with Highway 1. After turning onto a beautiful paved road, the rider will come to signs that say: ROAD CLOSED, NO THROUGH TRAFFIC. These signs are to prevent tourists from getting lost. The road is open but soon turns to dirt and gravel for about 5 miles. There are two steep sections here, but it is quite rideable on a road bike. And the views of valley and ocean are spectacular.

A few words of warning: During hunting season (six weeks in late August and September), and during "mud season" (usually December through March), Willow Creek probably should be avoided, and the alternate route through Monte Rio should be taken. Also, some of this road is open range, and there are occasionally cows on the road. Those riding mountain bikes should note that although there are tempting trails off Willow Creek, they are not legal.

The Occidental Cruise ends with a roller coaster, paved section on Willow Creek and then a rush of a descent back to

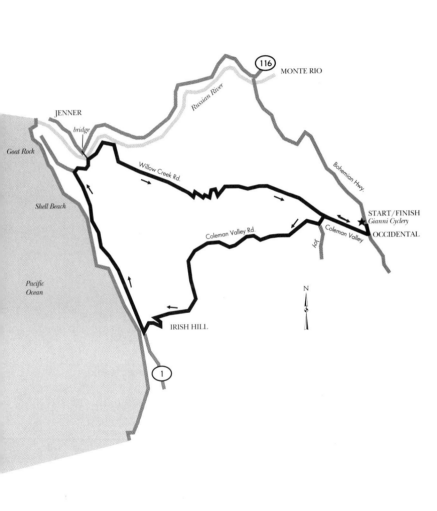

Occidental. We recommend you stop by Gianni and tell them how much you enjoyed the ride before checking out the Bohemian Cafe for dinner.

The Basics

Start: Gianni Cyclery, 3780 Bohemian Hwy., Occidental
Length: 28.6 miles.
Terrain: Rolling, steep descending; one major climb on dirt. The rural roads have no traffic. Hwy. 1 is fairly busy.
Food: In Occidental, there are a number of excellent restaurants, especially the Union Hotel, Negris, and the Bohemian Cafe. On the coast, water is available at campgrounds. At the base of Willow Creek, there is an Indian restaurant—The Sizzling Tandoor.
For more information: Gianni Cyclery, 3780 Bohemian Hwy., Occidental, CA 95465; (707) 874–2833.

Miles & Directions

- 0.0   From Gianni Cyclery, right on Bohemian Hwy.
- 0.2   Right on Coleman Valley Rd. Up the hill.
- 1.7   Bear left at the intersection of Willow Creek Rd. Stay on Coleman Valley.
- 1.9   Bear right at the intersection of Joy. Stay on Coleman Valley.
- 10.0   Right on Hwy. 1. Watch for traffic on weekends.
- 16.4   Right on Willow Creek Rd. Turns to dirt in approximately 2 miles. Continue on through major climbing.

(An alternate paved route would be to go right on Hwy. 116, right on Bohemian Hwy. to Occidental.)

- 26.9 Left on Coleman Valley. Down the hill to Occidental.
- 28.4 Left on Bohemian Hwy.
- 28.6 Ride ends at Gianni Cyclery.

South San Francisco Bay Area

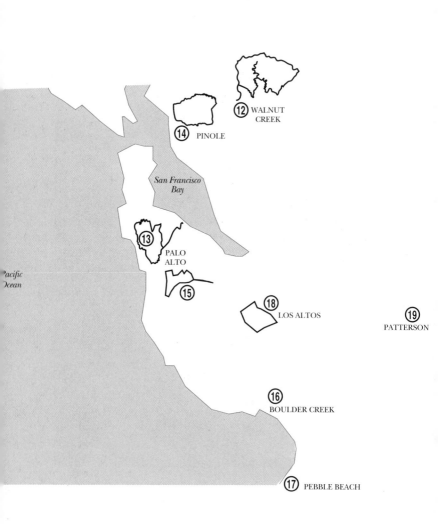

Pacific
Ocean

San Francisco
Bay

⑫ WALNUT
CREEK

⑭ PINOLE

⑬ PALO
ALTO

⑮

⑱ LOS ALTOS

⑲
PATTERSON

⑯ BOULDER CREEK

⑰ PEBBLE BEACH

South San Francisco Bay Area

12

Around and Over Diablo Classic

*Walnut Creek—Clayton—Morgan Territory—
Danville—Mt. Diablo State Park—Walnut Creek*

*God made the grass, the air and the rain; and the grass,
the air and the rain made the Irish; and the Irish turned
the grass, the air and the rain back into God.*
                              —Sean O'Faolain, *Holiday*

It's a common experience among California bike tourists. You're rolling beneath the shade of a dense forest when all of a sudden it opens to naked rolling hills. In one fell swoop you've been transported to Ireland. And you are there, gliding over fog-enshrouded hills, far away from everything American. Inevitable, inescapable fantasizing begins. You, on a short ride home to your castle. You, pedaling to the stone, ivy-covered mansion of your redheaded love—just like the main character in some glorified Irish Spring commercial. Even if you've never been to Ireland, the hills allow you to transport yourself, and your imagination is able to let loose.

Marin County's Point Reyes is California's obvious Ireland clone, but there are parts of Contra Costa County around the foothills of venerable Mt. Diablo that also evoke that Ireland/Scotland wish-fulfillment-via-fantasy thing. It's hard to believe that the Around and Over Diablo Classic ride could ever lead to anything pure if you judge it from its starting point in the quintessential suburb land of Walnut Creek. But after pedaling past the brand-new housing developments in Clayton at mile 8, you come to the place where 1990s Americana stops and the ageless beauty of the natural world begins.

Turn onto Marsh Creek Road, and you are rolling past farmland on a virtually empty stretch of tarmac, where you're more likely to see a tractor than a car. Modest farmhouses with horses grazing in the front yards are scattered about the open grasslands, and your path becomes even more bucolic as you turn onto Morgan Territory Road, where gentle old trees form a shaded archway over the narrow road.

After 18 miles the road gets even skinnier and more remote. Trees thicken around you. For much of this stretch, the road is one-lane, so watch out for the occasional car that may twist unexpectedly around one of the snaky bends.

A gradual climb out of the trees yields to the Ireland-evoking open space of the Morgan Territory Regional Preserve. Lumpy green hills massage the earth, and weary bicyclists may feel a sense of renewal just from riding amid the pure quiet of the softly rolling hills. The air is sweet and clean and quiet, as tall, waving grass ripples in the wind. In just 24 miles of pedaling you've completely removed yourself from the material trappings of suburbia.

At mile 24.6 you'll pass rows of perfectly white, perfectly organized high-tech windmills covering the hillside to your left. Shortly afterward the road widens to two lanes and becomes a flat, winding ribbon carrying you past quiet countryside. In the distance Mt. Diablo rises high above the hills, waiting to torture your legs with its steep, unrelenting grades.

When you reach the Danville city limits, you'll have 5 miles of suburban riding—including a cruise through the sticky-sweet gingerbread houses and tennis villas of Blackhawk Road—before turning onto Mt. Diablo Scenic Drive, which marks your entrance into Mt. Diablo State Park. From here you'll have nearly 10 miles of climbing before reaching Diablo's summit. And 10 miles of mountain climbing can feel like dragging an anvil when you've already done 50 miles, especially on a hot day, when temperatures on Diablo's unshaded tarmac can be brutal.

Once you're atop Mt. Diablo, the pain of the climb is superseded by the victory of the conquest. On a clear day you can see much of the Bay Area spread out before you. And as the wind blows through your sweaty hair, you can look forward to the promise of 11 miles of scenic descending as you mount your two-wheeled companion and make your way back to Walnut Creek. From the bottom of Diablo, which ends with a no-brakes straightaway that provides the perfect culmination to this epic descent, you're only 5 miles from downtown Walnut Creek. Restaurants range form ethnic to the standard Big Three (McDonald's, Burger King, and Wendy's). And if celebrating the completion of a 73-mile ride means embracing the suburban lifestyle with a Biggie Coke and Biggie Fries, by all means, go for it.

The Basics

Start: Main St. and Civic Dr. in downtown Walnut Creek.
Length: 72.9 miles.
Terrain: Much extended climbing, rolling hills, some flat sections; moderate traffic in suburbs and towns but virtually no traffic for the majority of the ride.
Food: Restaurants and stores available in Walnut Creek. No food or water available for 30 miles between Clayton and Danville. Water fountains, but no food, on Mt. Diablo.
For more information: Valley Spokesmen Bicycle Touring Club, P.O. Box 2630, Dublin, CA 94568; Bonnie Powers, (510) 828–5299. Water on top of Morgan

Miles & Directions

- 0.0 Civic Dr. and Main St.; go north on Civic Dr. You are in the middle of a very busy downtown.

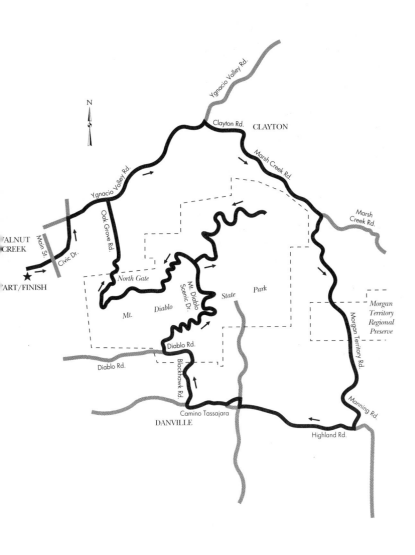

- 0.3 Right onto Ygnacio Valley Rd.; parallel bike path available.
- 4.2 Bike path ends; climb begins.
- 5.3 Summit.
- 7.8 Right onto Clayton Rd.
- 8.0 Clayton.
- 9.3 Right onto Marsh Creek Rd.
- 13.9 Right onto Morgan Territory Rd.
- 23.2 Morgan Territory Regional Preserve.
- 28.2 Alameda County line.
- 29.0 Right onto Manning Rd.
- 29.8 Right onto Highland Rd.
- 30.0 Contra Costa County line.
- 34.6 Right onto Camino Tassajara.
- 38.3 Danville town limits.
- 39.4 Right onto Blackhawk Rd.
- 43.0 Blackhawk Rd. becomes Diablo Rd.
- 43.1 Right onto Mt. Diablo Scenic Dr.; entrance to Mt. Diablo State Park.
- 43.9 Begin climbing.
- 50.1 Right to Mt. Diablo summit.
- 54.6 Summit; turnaround point.
- 59.1 Keep right at intersection, following North Gate.
- 67.1 Right onto Oak Grove Rd.
- 68.2 Left onto Ygnacio Valley Rd.
- 72.6 Left onto N. Main St.
- 72.9 Ride ends at Main St. and Civic Dr.

13

Sky Londa Cruise

*Downtown Palo Alto—Woodside—Old La Honda
Road—Sky Londa—Kings Mountain Road—
Woodside—Downtown Palo Alto*

*We think bicycles can save—if not the world—at least
the quality of our immediate environments.*
—1994 Bridgestone Catalogue

Palo Alto. Home to the brainy kids of Stanford University. Land of the meticulously manicured yard. Gateway to God's Country.

With brains, wealth, and beauty to its credit, it's not surprising that this idyllic setting is a full-on cycling mecca, where you can find many a pair of fashionably buffed legs, watch a never-ending parade of drool-evoking bikes, and discover myriad opportunities for awe-inspiring cycling. Being that this is merely a touch of all that Palo Alto and its surrounding areas have to offer, it's the perfect starting point for yet another killer ride.

A mix of coffee bars, restaurants, and bookstores complement Palo Alto's downtown area, where the Wheelsmith Bike Shop and Museum—voted one of the ten best bike shops in the country by *Bicycling* magazine—offers the ideal launching pad for your catapult into the surrounding hills.

From downtown Palo Alto the ride cruises through BMW and Jaguar country, meanders across Stanford University, and lofts you into the peaceful hills above Woodside, where you're immediately distanced from the confusion below. Easter green in the spring and classic brown in the summer, the hills are dotted with Christmas tree farms, horse ranches, and elegant estates hidden among oak, birch, and redwood. Truly one of the more lovely parts of the Bay Area, these forested back roads come alive with Technicolor grandeur when you tour them by bike.

Once you turn onto Old La Honda Road, all traffic ceases, the road narrows, and your payoff begins. This tiny wooded road wriggles upward through the hills but never gets too steep to handle as it climbs for 3.5 miles to Skyline Boulevard (Highway 35). Expect to see fellow cyclists spinning and grinning under the shade of the towering trees that engulf the road and make it an absolute sanctuary in the summer. Once a logging road, Old La Honda narrows as you get closer to the summit, snaking precariously above the valley until you finally reach the top.

When you reach Skyline, you'll get to experience the rush of a screaming descent as you barrel into Sky Londa, a sparse smattering of civilization nestled quietly amid the redwoods. For hungry, weary cyclists ready for some real down-home cooking, you'll find Alice's Restaurant—a favorite hangout of bikers of the motorized variety. And for a quick food fix, there's a general store right across the street.

The ride continues on busy Highway 35, but not for long. After 5.8 miles of rolling hills, you'll turn onto quiet Kings Mountain Road. As it rambles through cooling redwood groves, this amazing sliver of asphalt includes dozens of hairpin turns that help to spiral the road downward to the valley. It's a tricky descent, so be sure to exercise caution. On your way down Kings Mountain Road, don't go so fast that you miss Huddart Park, one of the Peninsula's best-kept secrets (until now!). Take a quick look around and make a mental note to come back for a day hike and picnic.

Back on level ground in Woodside, you'll cruise past numerous horse farms, encountering not only four-legged beasts but also those of the four-wheeled variety. Yep. You're back to civilization, with all its grotesque (and glorious) trappings. Stop in at the well-to-do Woodside Market for a final pit stop, where you can mingle with the beautiful people before heading back to Palo Alto. Once you're back in town, Gordon Biersch, at 640 Emerson, serves up homemade brew and great food.

The Basics

Start: Wheelsmith Bike Shop, Hamilton Ave. and Emerson St., downtown Palo Alto.

Length: 33.2 miles.

Terrain: Extended climbing on quiet backroads; moderate traffic between Woodside and Palo Alto.

Food: Myriad restaurants in Palo Alto; Alice's Restaurant and general store in Sky Londa; fancy restaurants and a grocery store in Woodside.

For more information: Western Wheelers Bicycle Club, P.O. Box 518, Palo Alto, CA 94302; Jim Evans, (415) 858–0936. Wheelsmith Bike Shop, 201 Hamilton Ave., Palo Alto, CA 94301; (650) 324–1919.

Miles & Directions

- 0.0   Wheelsmith Bike Shop, Hamilton Ave. and Emerson St. Head south on Emerson toward University Ave.
- 0.1   Left onto University Ave.
- 0.3   Cross El Camino Ave. University Ave. becomes Palm St.; enter Stanford University.
- 0.6   Right onto Arboretum.
- 1.0   Left onto Sand Hill Rd.
- 4.2   Cross Hwy. 280 overpass.
- 6.7   Sand Hill becomes Portola Rd. Continue straight.
- 6.9   Right onto Old La Honda Rd. Begin climb.
- 10.5   Summit. Right onto Skyline Blvd. (Hwy. 35).
- 12.0   Intersection of Hwy. 35 and Hwy. 84. Continue on Hwy. 35 past Alice's Restaurant.
- 14.7   Wunderlich County Park.

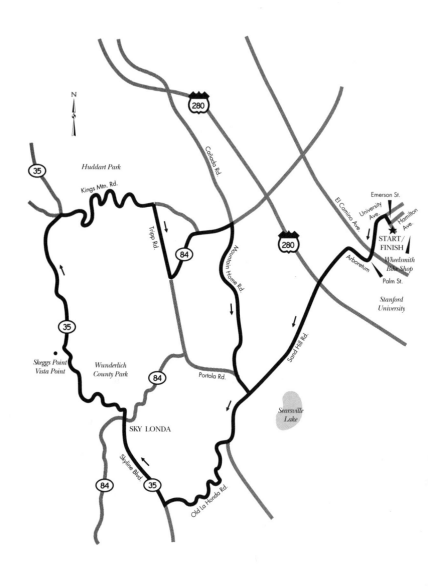

N

35

Huddart Park

Kings Mtn. Rd.

Tripp Rd.

84

35

Skeggs Point
Vista Point

Wunderlich
County Park

84

Portola Rd.

SKY LONDA

Skyline Blvd.

84

35

Old La Honda Rd.

Cañada Rd.

280

Mountain Home Rd.

280

Sand Hill Rd.

Searsville
Lake

El Camino Ave.

University
Ave.

Emerson St.

Hamilton
Ave.

START/
FINISH

Wheelsmith
Bike Shop

Arboretum

Palm St.

Stanford
University

- 16.0 Skeggs Point Vista Point.
- 17.8 Right onto Kings Mtn. Rd.
- 20.8 Huddart Park entrance.
- 22.3 Right at Woodside historical site, Tripp Rd.
- 23.1 Left onto Woodside Rd. (Hwy. 84).
- 24.4 Right onto Mountain Home Rd.
- 26.5 Left onto Portola Rd.
- 26.8 Left onto Sand Hill Rd.; retrace directions back to Palo Alto.
- 33.2 Ride ends at Wheelsmith Bike Shop.

14

Pinole Ramble

*Pinole—Hercules—Rodeo—Crockett—Carquinez
Scenic Drive—Carquinez Strait Regional Shoreline—
Martinez—Alhambra Valley Road—Pinole*

> *Thank goodness for cheap bicycles and the mass mer-
> chants who sell them. Inexpensive bicycles helped make
> childhood fun, and without them, lots of people would
> never have learned to ride a bike at all.*
>
> —1994 Bridgestone Catalogue

If you've got a bike (any bike will do) and you've got a body
(any ole body), then you've got everything you need to enjoy
this splendid ramble from the shores of the San Francisco Bay
to the orchards of the Alhambra Valley. Cyclists new to the
sport will love the Pinole Ramble as much as all the more experienced local riders who have made these delicious roads part of
their regular cycling feast. On any given day you're likely to see
everyone from the buffed-legs-and-fancy-bike set to the brand-
new-bike-from-Kmart crowd out on their two-wheeled vehicles
of choice, taking advantage of the less-traveled roads around
the Carquinez Strait and the Alhambra Valley.

Departing from the old downtown of Pinole, you'll find it
hard to believe that you'll soon be traveling amid golden grasslands, wild groves of blackberries, and rolling farm roads. Of
course, finding your way to these glorious Bay Area backroads
takes a bit of perseverance. You'll have to battle the minimalls
and golden arches of suburbia for 6 miles before your wheels

roll onto the promised land. Included in this 6-mile tour-o'-the-'burbs is a grotesquely fascinating sensory extravaganza at the Wickland Oil Terminal. As you pedal by this monstrous structure, you can hear its clanging factory sounds, sniff its malodorous fumes, and behold its ugly industrial towers of pollution. It's a disturbing contrast to the glistening bay on your left, but for some sick reason it's hard to pull your eyes away from it.

Thankfully, cold suburbs and industrial wastelands are a thing of the past as you spin into the neighboring community of Crockett at mile 6.4. This cafe-and-thrift-store type of town doesn't have the impersonal glare of towns like Rodeo and Pinole. In fact, it has a certain good-natured funk to it. And best of all, it symbolizes your departure from the suburbs and your entrance into the sublime.

In less than 1 mile, your ride becomes countrified as you begin pedaling on the Carquinez Scenic Drive. Because this route is not a through road for cars, you'll probably pass more walkers and cyclists than motorists.

As you wend through vast, undeveloped pasturelands, the threat of intense heat from this unshaded road is likely to be softened by cool air off the San Francisco Bay. As you rise and fall with the gentle pitches of road, the rush of wind and the expansive emptiness of the soft, lumpy hills are enough to evoke a near-perfect elation. The simple beauty of these grassy knolls that roll lazily to the shores of the Carquinez Strait serves as a reminder of what's really important in life.

When you encounter the road closure at mile 10.6, go around the gate and continue traveling on the Carquinez Scenic Drive. The road is washed out, making it dangerous for cars but quite passable by bicycle. The absence of autos makes this short section of the route mystifyingly quiet. The fluttering of birds overhead and perhaps the whir of another bicycle wheel are the only sounds you'll hear. Watch for chunks of missing asphalt that disintegrate into dirt, and broken bits of road just waiting to puncture your tires. Your chances of flatting here are relatively high, and you won't want to be without your requisite tube, patch kit, and pump.

Rejoining cars and development in Martinez, you'll have a short jaunt through town, where you can stop for a snack before rejoining nature on the inland farm roads of the Alhambra Valley. You'll roll past wild blackberry patches, as well as rows of carefully planned orchards with tantalizing fruit dangling from their limbs. The road billows up and over soft green hills, as it snakes its way back toward Pinole, careening past ranches and farms, and traversing alongside empty country meadows dotted with wildflowers.

After nearly 10 miles of pedaling on Alhambra Valley Road, you'll be reunited with the ever-lovin' fast-food restaurants and sacred shopping malls of America. But as you spin into Pinole, you'll be refueled with an insider's knowledge of the hidden beauty lying beyond the confines of these suburbs, the promise and hope inherent in an empty green hill or revealed in a patch of spontaneous wildflowers growing from the cracks of a quiet road. And this knowledge will carry you through until your next bike touring adventure.

The Basics

Start: San Pablo and Tennent Aves. intersection in downtown Pinole.

Length: 30.7 miles.

Terrain: Rolling hills, with a few extended climbs (no longer than 1 mile each). Quiet country roads for the majority of the ride.

Food: No grocery stores or restaurants at the ride start, but there's a big grocery store right on the bike route in the next town over, Hercules. After you've passed Crockett, there aren't any food options until you hit Martinez. From there you'll have the possibility of wild blackberries on Alhambra Valley Rd., but don't eat the farmers' fruit from their orchards, as tempting as it may be.

For more information: Valley Spokesmen Bicycle Touring Club, Box 2630, Dublin, CA 94568; Bonnie Powers, (510) 828–5299.

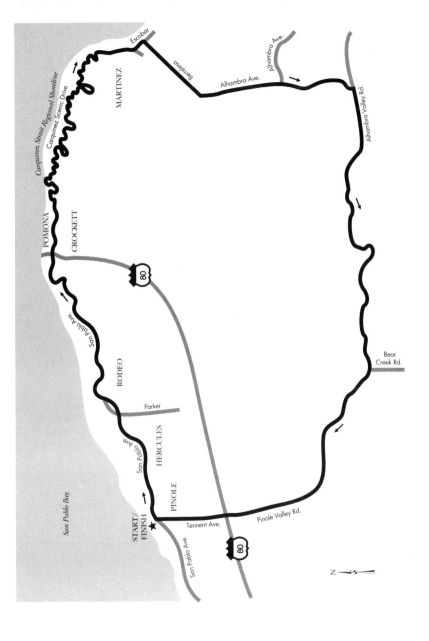

Miles & Directions

- 0.0 San Pablo Ave. and Tennent Ave. in old downtown Pinole. Turn right (east) onto San Pablo Ave. toward Hercules.
- 0.4 Hercules city limits.
- 2.3 Left onto Parker.
- 2.4 Rodeo city limits.
- 3.3 Parker becomes San Pablo Ave.
- 4.6 Wickland Oil Terminal. Begin climb.
- 5.5 Summit.
- 6.0 Crockett; San Pablo Ave. becomes Pomona.
- 6.1 Veer right; follow sign TO CARQUINEZ SCENIC DRIVE.
- 6.4 Downtown Crockett.
- 7.2 Begin Carquinez Scenic Dr.
- 8.3 Carquinez Strait Regional Shoreline.
- 10.6 Road closed (passable by bike).
- 14.5 St. Catherine of Siena Cemetery.
- 14.6 Carquinez Scenic Dr. becomes Talbart.
- 14.8 Turn left onto Escobar.
- 14.9 Right onto Berrelesa, which becomes Alhambra Ave.
- 16.9 Cross under Hwy. 4.
- 17.4 Right onto Alhambra Valley Rd.
- 18.7 Right at stop sign, continuing on Alhambra Valley Rd.
- 23.7 Intersect with Bear Creek Rd.; continue on Alhambra Valley Rd. to Pinole.
- 27.5 Pinole city limits. Alhambra Valley Rd. becomes Pinole Valley Rd.
- 30.0 Cross under Hwy. 80.
- 30.2 Pinole Valley Rd. becomes Tennent Ave.
- 30.7 Ride ends at Tennent Ave. and San Pablo Ave.

15

Bay to Coast Classic

Palo Alto—Sam McDonald Park—Pescadero—
San Gregorio—Palo Alto

Life is an uphill struggle. . . . you'd better train!
—Dave Stahl

One great thing about the Bay Area is the opportunity to go from one world to another in a matter of a few miles. This is most obvious in the meteorological sense. The Bay Area is famous for its climatic zones. But it's equally true that you can go from one world to another culturally and aesthetically.

This ride starts in the heart of Silicon Valley, at Page Mill and Foothill. Just up the road in one direction is Xerox Corporation, and in the other is the Stanford Linear Accelerator. But after a few miles of riding, you leave this world behind and begin to ascend Page Mill, known as "The Mill" to generations of cyclists. Below, the valley and the San Francisco Bay spread out, some days in azure splendor, other days under a blanket of fog. This is definitely low-gear territory, and The Mill can be both exhilarating and a grind, especially on the exposed upper sections.

For the Bay to Ocean Classic, cyclists should bring clothing for a wide range of possible weather scenarios. Typically, an early-morning start is greeted with fog at the bottom of the climb and then sun above 1,000 feet. On the ocean side, fog and even rain are possible and can occur on a warm summer day, and temperatures may range thirty degrees.

Going over the crest of Skyline Road and down West Alpine you will emerge from the redwoods into open meadows with a commanding 100-mile view of the Pacific. Farther down, you enter the redwoods again, now on a twisting, dark, and slippery road through Sam McDonald Park. Take it easy here—in fact, it's a nice place to stop to rest your descending muscles.

Afterward on Pescadero Road, watch out for the RIDE SINGLE FILE signs. These are probably not legal, but the locals think they are.

Pescadero Road comes out in the town of Pescadero, an ocean-side community with a weather-beaten look. A stop at the Arcangeli Bakery for the three-pound cinnamon roll is highly recommended. Bread is baked on the premises, and it's always tempting to take home a loaf (but how?). This is a great place to relax and contemplate the day, and if you sit very long on the bench out front, you are sure to meet other cyclists.

From Pescadero, Stage Road winds along the bluffs overlooking the Pacific, a gorgeous seaside road with no traffic. The Peterson and Alsford General Store in San Gregorio is another great place to stop, particularly for a cup of coffee, made fresh by the cup. Stage ends with a small climb to Highway 1, which is followed by a short but exhilarating 50-mile-per-hour descent into Tunitas Creek canyon, offering a great view of the surf breaking on the rocks below.

Tunitas is a classic Santa Cruz Mountains climb that starts gradually in open, windswept artichoke fields, gradually steepens into deep redwoods, and finally levels off as it follows the ridge top to Skyline. This isolated road is known for its wildlife, especially for deer, foxes, and bobcats.

Once at the top, it's a fast and tricky descent down Kings Mountain Road to Woodside. But a right turn on Skyline to Highway 84 provides two smooth and banked descents that require much less braking. A right turn on Portola Road will place you on the route of the Noon Ride, and if it's around 12:30 P.M. on a weekday, you can wave at the racers as they charge past in the opposite direction.

The Basics

Start: Page Mill and Foothill, Palo Alto. Parking is available on Old Page Mill Rd. or at the Park and Ride on Page Mill and I–280.
Length: 65 miles.
Terrain: Prolonged descending and climbing. Roads are traffic free, and road surfaces are generally good. Rough spots on West Alpine Rd.
Food: Try the Arcangeli Bakery in Pescadero and The Peterson and Alsford General Store in San Gregorio. There is a grocery and Alice's Restaurant in Sky Londa.
For more information: The Bicycle Outfitter, 963 Fremont Ave., Los Altos, CA 94022; (650) 948–6841.

Miles & Directions

- 0.0   Page Mill/Old Page Mill Rd. and Foothill in Palo Alto. West on Old Page Mill Rd.
- 1.0   Merge with Page Mill.
- 1.5   Pass under I–280.
- 2.0   Begin climbing.
- 10.0   Skyline. Go straight across. You are now on West Alpine Rd.
- 17.0   West Alpine ends at Pescadero. Turn left. Sam McDonald Park.
- 18.5   Summit of Haskins Hill on Pescadero. Watch for traffic on Pescadero Road.
- 28.5   Pescadero. Right onto Stage. Arcangeli Bakery.
- 35.5   San Gregorio. The Peterson and Alsford General Store. Continue straight on Stage.
- 37.0   Right on Hwy. 1. Fast descent.
- 38.5   Right on Tunitas Creek Rd.
- 40.0   Begin climbing on Tunitas Creek.

- 47.5 Right on Skyline. Fast descent on Skyline.
- 53.0 Left on Hwy. 84. Sky Londa. Fast descent on Hwy. 84.
- 56.0 Right on Portola Rd.
- 57.0 Right at intersection. This is still Portola.
- 60.5 Left on Alpine.
- 61.5 Right on Arastradero.
- 63.5 Left on Page Mill.
- 64.0 Left onto Old Page Mill Rd.
- 65.0 Ride ends at Page Mill and Foothill.

16

Boulder Creek Challenge

*Santa Cruz—Boulder Creek—Zayante—Felton—
Henry Cowell State Park—Santa Cruz*

> *With my bike, I have the courage and resolve to go to
> places I've never been. And then, without noticing, the bi-
> cycle trip becomes a point of departure for other things.
> It's all part of the lure and magic of the road.*
> —Elaine Mariolle, *California Bicyclist*

Serendipity. It's that unexpected bonus life throws at us every
now and then. Like finding $10 in the pocket of a jersey you
haven't worn in months. Or meeting your future spouse on a
century ride.

It's not surprising that bike fanatics experience these
serendipitous moments more often than the rest of the world.
Every time you mount your metal stallion, you're pedaling off
on a new adventure, and the things that greet you around the
bend or over a summit are often unexpected, sometimes amazing, and—every once in a while—life-changing.

Riding into the tiny mountain town of Boulder Creek is an
experience of serendipitous proportions. From the cozy community of Santa Cruz, you can look toward the tree-enshrouded
mountains and easily envision yourself pedaling up secluded
roads through corridors of redwoods. As you look hillward and
think about your ride, beautiful terrain seems almost a given.
But on these quiet, forested roads, what you probably *don't* expect to find is the sandal-wearin', tofu-munchin' town of Boul-

der Creek, which appears out of nowhere like some time-warped, psychedelic mirage. The town is a modern-day refuge for real-life hippies—old and young alike—who loll cross-legged on the sidewalks surrounded by mountains and sheltered from the harshness of today's world. You almost expect to see a tie-dyed cloud hovering in the air above.

Although the city of Santa Cruz retains some of its hippie roots, the true believers have fled to the mountains of Boulder Creek. And on your bike from downtown, it'll be a hilly 24 miles to visit them up there. The climbing begins almost immediately as you head toward UC Santa Cruz and are immediately engulfed by a sea of redwoods. It's a gradual uphill grind that lasts for 15 miles but is made a bit easier by the generally gentle grade of the road and the ever-changing landscape—which keeps your mind off the dull pain of throbbing legs. From the top, distant mountains provide the perfect backdrop for the kind of picturesque ridge riding that makes you wonder whether you should laugh, cry, or hop off your bike and drop to the ground for a moment of reverence.

If you're not into the peace, love, and organic food scene in Boulder Creek, there's yet another good reason to stop here: The climbing isn't over yet for this ride, and this will be your last chance to get water and food for at least 23 miles. From Boulder Creek, 5 scenic and secluded miles lie between you and your next climb. By the time Bear Creek Road begins to arch and pull its way up the mountain, you're enveloped in a forest as thick and wild and brown and moist as something you'd find in the Amazon. You are not, however, anywhere near the Amazon, and the small and unassuming wineries that are tucked into the folds of the forest serve as a locale reminder. The unique climate and terrain of Northern California make it one of the few places in the world that redwood trees can call home and in which vineyards can prosper.

When you pass the Byington Winery at mile 32.1, you're almost home free. From here it's less than 1 mile before the road coils into a spiraling descent. It's not exactly mindless cruising, however. The road, which snakes narrowly down the mountain, with little room for more than one car, requires some concentration and a lot of good technique in order to get the most enjoyment out of it (and to prevent crashing).

There's nothing but nature for 14 plummeting, plunging miles as you work your way out of the mountains and back toward town. From Felton, city life begins to thicken all around you. After you've passed the north boundary of Henry Cowell State Park, it'll be you and the cars dropping back into Santa Cruz. But this isn't necessarily a bad thing. As you descend, smell the lattes. Envision a deli sandwich and a sidewalk cafe. Click your heels three times and say "There's no place like home." You're almost there.

The Basics

Start: Spokesman Bicycles at Cathcart St. and Cedar St. in downtown Santa Cruz.

Length: 53.4 miles.

Terrain: Major climbs, steep descents, virtually no flat sections. Secluded roads, often one-lane. Heavy traffic for 3 miles on Hwy. 236.

Food: There are plenty of food options in Santa Cruz, of course. The Jahva House in downtown Santa Cruz offers terrific coffee as well as an interesting, light menu and is also a good introduction to the denizens of Santa Cruz. The Jahva House is located at 120 Union between Center St. and Cedar St. A market and a restaurant are in Boulder Creek at mile 24.2. After that, no food or water is available until Felton, at mile 47.2. (In desperation, you may be able to find a hose in someone's yard.)

For more information: Santa Cruz Visitors Information Center, 701 Front St., Santa Cruz, CA 95061; (408) 425–1234. Spokesman Bicycles, 231 Cathcart St., Santa Cruz, CA 95060; (408) 429–6062.

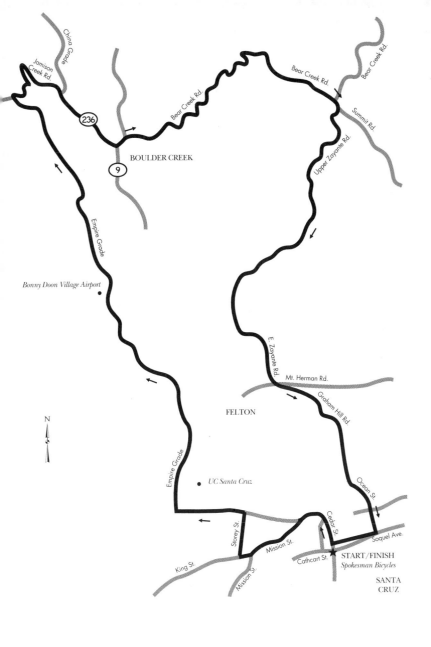

Miles & Directions

- 0.0   From Spokesman Bicycles on Cathcart St. at Cedar St. in downtown Santa Cruz, take a right onto Cedar.
- 0.4   Right onto Center St.; then an immediate left onto Mission St.
- 0.7   Right onto King St.
- 0.8   Right onto Storey St.
- 1.0   Left onto High St. to UC Santa Cruz; begin climbing.
- 2.0   Pass UC Santa Cruz on your right.
- 3.3   Road narrows, High St. becomes Empire Grade.
- 11.8 Pass Bonny Doon Village Airport.
- 17.0 Descent begins.
- 18.4 Right onto Jamison Creek Rd.; major descent!
- 21.5 Right on Hwy. 236 (unmarked). Heavy traffic; no shoulder.
- 24.2 Boulder Creek. Left onto Hwy. 9.
- 24.5 Right onto Bear Creek Rd.
- 29.4 Begin climb.
- 32.1 Pass Byington Winery.
- 33.7 Descent begins. *Careful:* Very twisty!
- 34.7 Right onto Summit Rd.; one-lane road.
- 34.9 Right onto Upper Zayante Rd.
- 38.8 Continue straight through intersection.
- 43.5 Stop sign; continue straight.
- 47.2 Felton. Right onto Mt. Herman Rd. Left onto Graham Hill Rd.
- 48.1 Pass north boundary of Henry Cowell State Park.
- 51.6 Veer right onto Ocean St.
- 52.0 Cross under Hwy. 101; veer right, following Ocean St.
- 52.8 Right onto Soquel Ave.
- 53.2 Right onto Pacific.
- 53.3 Left onto Cathcart St.
- 53.4 Ride ends at Spokesman Bicycles on Cathcart at Cedar.

Pebble Beach Cruise

Monterey—17 Mile Drive—Pebble Beach—
Pacific Grove—Monterey

> *There is a beautiful view from the Carmel grade, the*
> *curving bay with the waves creaming on the sand, the*
> *dune country around Seaside and right at the bottom of*
> *the hill, the warm intimacy of the town.*
> —John Steinbeck, *Cannery Row*

The natural attributes of Monterey and its surrounding areas
have become more developed since the days of Steinbeck, but
its stunning beauty has somehow survived. Monterey is a salty
canvas of windswept lines and crashing waves and gentle grades
leading to limitless seascape vistas. As you pedal away from the
crowds of the downtown area, the dramatic coastal landscape is
enough to trigger that rare, euphoric feeling of being in the best
of all possible places in the best of all possible ways—on your
bike.

With the vast scope of things to see and do, the 28-mile Pebble Beach Cruise is the kind of ride that could take all day. And
maybe it should. Leave your Greg LeMond attitude behind, and
instead heft along your trusty camera. This is one ride you
won't want to remember as a blur.

Your ride starts right outside Monterey at the Sand Dunes
Beach parking lot. All you'll find here is a parking lot, a beach,
and a bike path, but then, that's all you need, right? Besides,
within 3 miles of the ride's start, you'll reach downtown Mon-

terey, Fisherman's Wharf, Cannery Row, and every amenity—including "I Love Monterey" baseball caps and cotton candy—that you ever dreamed possible. The bustling, working-class wharf of the Cannery Row that John Steinbeck made famous now exists only in the text of his classic tale. Authenticity has made way for capitalism, resulting in a 1990s tourism amalgam of McDonald's eateries, trained monkeys, and street mimes.

If you can endure—maybe even get a kick out of—2 miles of true tackiness, the crowded bike path will begin to thin out and lead you to Ocean View Drive, one of the most sensational stretches of beach on the entire California coastline. As you cruise up the coast, make sure to unglue your eyes from the ocean long enough to check out the other side of the road, where virtually tame deer frolic on the famed Pebble Beach Golf Course.

After almost 4 miles of ocean, the road curves gently inland and brings you to the start of the 17 Mile Drive, which is chock-full of amazing vista points and gently rolling roads shaded by arching trees. Because this "drive" is one of the biggest tourist attractions in the entire area, you'll have to succumb to bureaucratic rigmarole by checking in with a ranger and signing a waiver stating that you'll be a good bicyclist and follow the rules and stay on designated roads. Although this stretch of tarmac is definitely not the stuff of secluded backroads, the overpowering grandeur of the surrounding land and sea makes it well worth the relatively minor hassle of sharing the road with car-driving tourists. And once you've experienced the two-wheeled version of this drive, with the salty wind whipping in your face and the rollercoaster hills pulling you effortlessly forward, you'll feel truly sorry for all those tourists cooped up in their mechanized boxes. By trading your Big Gulp and car stereo for a windbreaker and a Power Bar, you get to experience the 17 Mile Drive in a way that no car driver ever will.

The only major climb of the day comes as the road forks with an option of heading up to Highway 1 or dropping down into the overpriced, overcommercialized "hamlet" of Carmel. Your ride heads upward, past a cautionary sign that basically warns bicyclists that the hill ahead is going to kick their butts. The climb *is* steep, but if you've done this ride right, you've made lots of stops along the way to groove on the scenery, and you should be thoroughly rested for this 1.5-mile challenge. After you crest the hill and get onto Highway 1, you'll be on your way back to Monterey. Retrace your tread past glorious Ocean View Drive, congested Fisherman's Wharf, and, finally, back to the soft, squishy sound of waves against sand at Sand Dunes Beach.

The Basics

Start: Sand Dunes Beach parking lot. Exit Hwy. 1 at the Canyon Del Ray exit. Proceed under the freeway overpass to Sand Dunes Beach, across from the Monterey Beach Hotel. No restrooms in parking lot.

Length: 28 miles.

Terrain: Long, flat stretches and gently rolling hills. One major climb toward the end of the ride. Ultrascenic drives with fair amounts of traffic on weekends.

Food: No food mart at the ride's start, but food options galore in downtown Monterey. Restaurants at the Pebble Beach Resort if you're feeling fancy. For a hearty dinner at a moderate price, you might check out Rosines on Alvarado St. in downtown Monterey.

For more information: Winning Wheels, 223 15th St., Pacific Grove, CA 93950; (408) 375–4322.

Miles & Directions

- 0.0 From parking lot, ride under freeway overpass onto Canyon Del Ray.
- 0.1 Turn right onto bike path parallel to Del Monte.
- 0.9 Cross Roberts Ave.; begin Monterey Peninsula Recreation Trail.

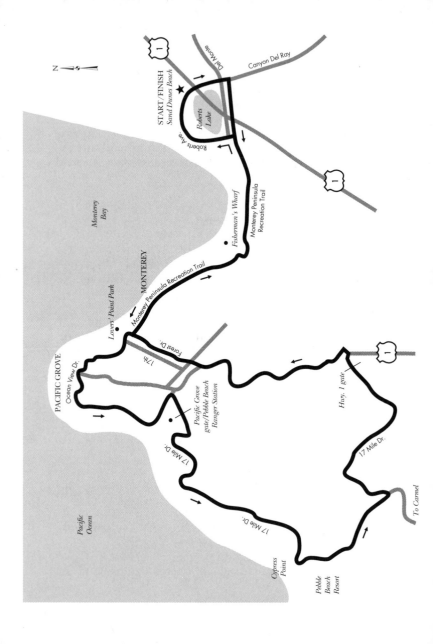

- 2.6 Stay on bike path through Fisherman's Wharf; highly congested area.
- 4.7 End bike path; turn right onto Ocean View Dr. past Lovers' Point Park.
- 8.3 Right onto 17 Mile Dr.
- 8.5 Pebble Beach Ranger Station; bicyclists *must* sign in.
- 9.5 Turn right, following 17 MILE DRIVE signs.
- 11.5 Continue on 17 Mile Dr.; don't follow BIKE ROUTE signs.
- 12.5 Veer right, following 17 MILE DRIVE signs.
- 13.1 Cypress Point lookout.
- 14.2 Path to the famous and oft-photographed Lone Cypress.
- 15.4 Turn right, following 17 Mile Dr. route
- 15.8 Pebble Beach Resort.

(At this point you may wish to follow an alternate route by retracing your steps along 17 Mile Dr. Returning this way is longer than taking Hwy. 68 but has less traffic.)

- 15.9 Turn right, following 17 Mile Dr. route.
- 17.5 Begin steep ascent up to Hwy. 1.
- 18.9 Left at Hwy. 1 gate, then another immediate left onto Hwy. 68 toward Pacific Grove.
- 23.2 Left onto Forest Dr. to Lovers' Point Park. Cross Ocean View Dr. Right onto bike path.
- 27.4 Left at Comfort Inn onto Roberts Ave.
- 27.7 Left onto Canyon Del Ray.
- 28.0 End at Sand Dunes Beach parking lot.

18

Black Mountain Cruise

Los Altos—Montebello Open Space Preserve—Los Altos

> *At one section on the climb, there were several bikes strung out ahead of me, front wheels flicking back and forth, zigzagging in the sunshine like a school of salmon struggling upstream.*
>
> —Rob Schott

Whoa! Check out the view! San Jose is a less than inspiring town to ride a bike through, but it's a great place to ride above. And the Black Mountain Cruise gives you the opportunity to do just this, providing a 360-degree view that includes Silicon Valley as well as the Pacific Ocean, Mount Tamalpais, Mount Diablo, Mount Hamilton, and even a glimpse of the snowy Sierras.

The ride starts at Bicycle Outfitter on the Foothill Expressway in Los Altos. If you hang out on Foothill for any length of time, you'll realize that you've come to road bike heaven, as a steady stream of racers, tourists, and commuters file past. The cruise goes south on Foothill to Stevens Canyon Reservoir, where there are bathrooms.

The 5-mile climb up Montebello starts with a series of steep switchbacks, before entering a stream canyon. Note the Sunrise Winery and Picchetti Ranch near the bottom of the climb. Road gradients on this part of Montebello approach 15 percent.

For the final 2 miles of the climb, you are rewarded with spectacular views of San Jose and the bay. After a storm, this view will be crystal clear, and on these days you can see the blimp hangars at Moffett Field. Often, however, the valley will have a morning blanket of fog. After 2,100 feet of climbing, the ride reaches the end of the pavement and a gate. Guide your bike through the narrow opening of the gate, and you're in the Montebello Open Space Preserve.

The road here is a mixture of degraded pavement and packed dirt that winds through scrub pine and manzanita thickets. It is easy riding until the final short climb to the top of Black Mountain (2,787 feet). This last quarter mile will require that you keep your weight over your back wheel for traction.

The Montebello Open Space Preserve is a great area for mountain biking, with many trails going off in all directions, so expect to see some mountain bikers on this ride. If you are on your skinny tires, just act as if riding on the dirt is the most natural thing in the world. They'll get over it. If you're on a mountain bike, you may want to explore Stevens Canyon by descending Indian Creek Trail.

At the top of Black Mountain, you'll find an outcropping of rock on your left that is a prime viewing point for the Pacific Ocean. It's a great place to stretch out and watch the sun set over the grassy hillsides that seem to stretch forever. Below, in Stevens Canyon, runs the San Andreas Fault. For this ride, don't forget your camera.

The rest of the way to Page Mill is downhill and somewhat loose, requiring caution on a road bike. You may want to bring along some additional clothing, as the weather can turn cold and breezy at the top, especially in the evening.

Once you reach the pavement of Page Mill and Moody Road, you are on a typically difficult Santa Cruz Mountains decent, with one switchback after another. The top of Moody is especially hard on the neck and hands, but it then opens out into a beautiful little valley before bringing you back to the Foothill Expressway. If you are in need of refreshments, there's a Starbucks, a Sonoma Country Bagel, and an Andronico's grocery at the corner of Foothill and Springer.

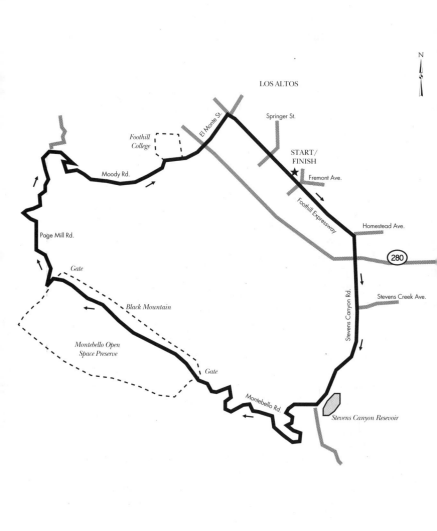

N

LOS ALTOS

Springer St.

El Monte St.

Foothill
College

Moody Rd.

START/
FINISH

Fremont Ave.

Foothill Expressway

Homestead Ave.

Page Mill Rd.

280

Gate

Black Mountain

Stevens Creek Ave.

Stevens Canyon Rd.

Montebello Open
Space Preserve

Gate

Montebello Rd.

Stevens Canyon Resevoir

The Basics

Start: Bicycle Outfitter, Foothill Expressway and Fremont Ave. in Los Altos.
Length: 27 miles.
Terrain: Major climbing on Montebello. Four miles of dirt. Twisty downhill on Page Mill Rd. and Moody Rd.
Food: The shopping center on the corner of Springer St. and Foothill Expressway has an Andronico's Market, as well as Starbucks Coffee and Sonoma Country Bagels.
For more information: Bicycle Outfitter, 963 Fremont Ave., Los Altos, CA 94022; (650) 948–6841.

Miles & Directions

- 0.0 Bicycle Outfitter, Foothill Expressway and Fremont Ave., Los Altos. Left (south) on Foothill Expressway.
- 2.5 Pass under I–280.
- 4.5 Foothill becomes Stevens Canyon Rd.
- 6.5 Right on Montebello Rd., just past Stevens Canyon Reservoir.
- 11.5 Gate at the end of the pavement on Montebello.
- 14.0 Black Mountain.
- 16.0 Right on Page Mill Rd. Careful on descent.
- 20.0 Right on Moody Rd. Careful on the Moody downhill.
- 23.0 Foothill College. Go through the college at Elena and reconnect with El Monte St. on the other side. The road is marked here. Left on El Monte.
- 24.5 Right on Foothill Expressway.
- 27.0 Ride ends at Bicycle Outfitter. Take the offramp before the underpass.

19

Del Puerto Canyon Challenge

Patterson—San Antonio Junction—Patterson

On a bicycle your destination is where you are.
—David Perry, *Bike Cult*

Interstate 5 runs the length of California's Central Valley, mostly skirting the western hills, away from the population centers of Fresno, Merced, and Modesto, and passing near previously obscure towns like Buttonwillow, Coalinga, and Patterson. Bike riding? There's not much here. Mostly it's bare hills, the flat valley floor, and a lot of wind.

But at Patterson, the attentive map reader will notice a road that snakes up through the hills to eventually climb the backside of Mt. Hamilton and descend into Silicon Valley. Del Puerto Canyon Road is the name of this thoroughfare, and it is an undiscovered gem for cyclists.

Most of Del Puerto Canyon Road follows Del Puerto Creek and consists of sweeping turns that reveal open side canyons with names like Windmill Canyon, Garden Canyon, and Murderers Canyon. On either side of the stream, the rounded, grassy hills rise 1,000 feet. A few broken-down cattle ranches that look like they've been there for a century are tucked away in the bottom land.

In this part of the canyon, you are riding through what geologists call the Great Valley sequence, a series of sedimentary sandstones and conglomerates roughly seventy million years old. It is the erosion of these rocks that give the hills their velvety look.

If you ride Del Puerto on a hot summer evening, the lower canyon has a feeling of total serenity. It's the perfect stop for a cycling ramble off of I-5. When you get tired or it starts getting dark, simply turn around and coast back to your start.

Halfway up Del Puerto, the route passes Frank Raines Park, where there is camping and water. On one side of the road is a charming roadside picnic area, and on the other an off-road vehicle park. After this, Del Puerto begins to steepen, with sharper curves and fallen rock on the pavement. The geology has now changed into metamorphosed oceanic rocks that have been thrust into place by plate tectonics. A large quartz vein at mile 17 is especially noteworthy. Generally there is no traffic on this ride, but cyclists should take care when rounding blind corners to stay on their side of the road.

After crossing the bridge at Peachtree Creek, climbing on Del Puerto begins in earnest, with 900 feet being covered in a little over 2 miles. The summit is at the Santa Clara county line (yes, the same county that San Jose is in), and then there is a short downhill to San Antonio Valley Road and the famous Junction Cafe, the only drinking establishment for 25 miles. Stop here for lunch on the picnic tables outside, or visit the pool tables inside and grab a bite to eat. And they do see cyclists, so they won't be surprised when you come dragging in.

The best way to return is to do Del Puerto in reverse. If you feel ambitious, however, you might undertake a side trip up Mt. Hamilton to the Lick Observatory and its magnificent view of the Bay Area. Be warned, however, it's another 20 miles and 3,000 feet of hard climbing. But the San Antonio Valley is worth a visit, especially in the spring when the poppies are in bloom.

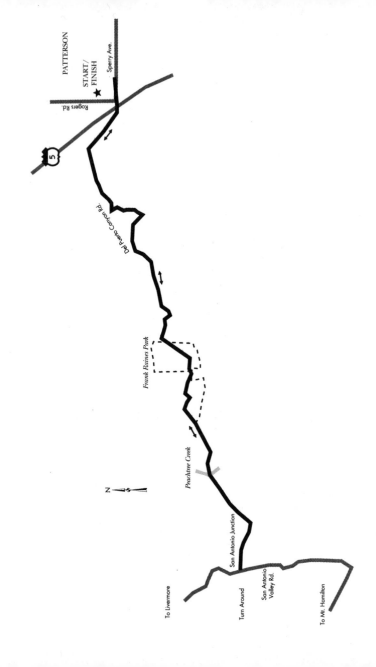

The Basics

Start: Sperry Ave. and Rogers Rd., at the Patterson exit from I-5. There is a mall being developed at this location, so there should be plenty of parking.

Length: 48 miles, but since it's an out-and-back, it can be cut short.

Terrain: Gradual climbing that becomes steep at the end. Smooth road. Cattle grates and occasional fallen rocks.

Food: The Junction Cafe at San Antonio Valley Rd. At the start, there are various fast-food restaurants.

For more information: Livermore Cyclery, 2288 1st St., Livermore, CA 94550; (510) 455–8090. The Patterson Apricot Fiesta is held in May of each year; (209) 892–3118.

Miles & Directions

- 0.0   Sperry Ave. and Rogers Rd. at the Patterson exit from I-5. Right (west) on Sperry and under the I-5 overpass.
- 19.0   Peachtree Creek. Steep climbing begins.
- 24.0   San Antonio Junction Rd. (This is an out-and-back ride.)

(If you wish to go to Mt. Hamilton, turn left on San Antonio Junction Rd., and proceed for 19 miles through the San Antonio Valley and up the mountain.)

Gold Country/Sierras

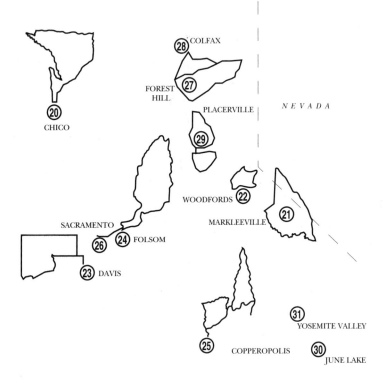

CHICO ⑳

⑳ CHICO

⑱ COLFAX

㉗ FOREST HILL

PLACERVILLE

㉙

N E V A D A

WOODFORDS ㉒

MARKLEEVILLE ㉑

SACRAMENTO

㉖ ㉔ FOLSOM

㉓ DAVIS

㉕ COPPEROPOLIS

㉛ YOSEMITE VALLEY

㉚ JUNE LAKE

Gold Country/Sierras

20

Chico to Paradise Challenge

Chico—Paradise—Honey Run Road—
Bidwell Park—Chico

> *The cyclist-beer connection is undeniable. The true sign*
> *one has fully adapted to the cycling lifestyle is the endless*
> *quest for new and different beers, preferably of the micro-*
> *brewed variety.*
> —Henry Kingman, *California Bicyclist*

The remote town of Chico is perhaps best known for the media attention its university has garnered as one of the country's top-ranking party schools. You'll find the hamlet nestled amid fiery canyons and undulating country roads—so seemingly unassuming, yet home to Chico State University, the bad boy of California's higher education system. The small town revolves around the school, and the school has given Chico somewhat of a . . . reputation. There's no doubt that images of raucous frat boys and pitchers of cheap, flat beer have discouraged more than one timid bike tourist or family-values type from planning a bike excursion in the area.

But don't let the media fool you. Cyclists in the know have long flocked to Chico for its small-town charm, quiet country roads, and, of course, to hoist a few cool ones at the Sierra Nevada Brewery, which churns out one of the best local beers in the state. One look around at all the buffed legs and cool bikes in Chico and you'll understand why some visiting cyclists love it so much that they never left.

Your ride begins in downtown Chico at The Bike Lane, 346 Broadway, a charming shop that is very helpful to cyclo-tourists. (Riders wishing to explore other interesting bike shops will find five of these within 3 blocks of their starting point. Chico is a very bike-friendly town.) To fuel up before embarking, we recommend a visit to Chico Natural Foods on Main Street and Seventh St.

The Chico to Paradise Challenge is blessed with all the qualities that make for a perfect ride: the peace and solitude of less-traveled roads, varying terrain, incredible scenery, and a swooping descent that twists down one of the most gorgeous roads in all of America. But if you're visiting Chico in the summer, you'll want to do this ride in the early morning or late afternoon: Temperatures can easily soar above one hundred degrees in the warm months.

The first half of your ride is pancake-flat. You'll coast through shaded orchards and open farmland as the distant canyonlands draw nearer. With each passing mile their fiery hues become more brilliant—and their summits appear all the steeper.

After 19 miles of relative coasting, the climbing begins. If you can handle the 4-mile uphill grind, you'll be rewarded in Paradise—literally. The climb ends in a tiny hilltop town that carries this only slightly euphemistic name.

From there you'll follow rollercoaster hills to Honey Run Road, where a descent of mind-blowing proportions awaits. This 6-mile plummet is the granddaddy of highlights in a ride chock-full of minihighlights. The road leads to a covered bridge at Butte Creek, and you're likely to find other cyclists hanging out and taking in the view here before heading back to the confines of civilization. From the bridge it's a quick ride to the wooded trails of Bidwell Park, which will lead you back to downtown Chico and The Bike Lane. Here all the creature comforts necessary to fully bask in après-ride glow are right around the corner.

Incidentally, for those cyclists who do this ride during the week, the Chico Farmers' Market is in full swing every Thursday night (when it's not raining) on Broadway, right in front of The Bike Lane. With great food and entertainment, this event shouldn't be missed.

The Basics

Start: The Bike Lane, 4th St. and Broadway, in downtown Chico.

Length: 46.5 miles.

Terrain: 19 miles of flat farmland on quiet country roads. One extended climb; one lengthy descent.

Food: Chico Natural Foods offers a great selection of organic produce and healthful snacks. Butte County Store at 14.1 miles has energy bars and more snacks. There is a convenience store on the route in Paradise. Back in Chico the food options abound.

For more information: Chico Velo Cycling Club, P.O. Box 2285, Chico, CA 95927; (530) 343–VELO. The Bike Lane, 346 Broadway, Chico, CA 95928; (530) 345–2453.

Miles & Directions

- 0.0 From The Bike Lane, 4th St. and Broadway, take Broadway south to Park Avenue.
- 1.5 Park Ave. and East Park Ave. intersect. Continue straight; Park Ave. becomes The Midway.
- 3.9 Veer left onto Oroville-Chico Hwy. *Careful:* It's easy to miss.
- 8.9 Oroville-Chico Hwy. ends at Durham-Dayton Hwy. Left onto Durham-Dayton Hwy.
- 9.4 Cross over Hwy. 99; becomes Durham-Pentz Rd.
- 13.2 Butte College.
- 14.1 Cross Clark Rd. (Hwy. 191) to Butte County Store: Stock up on food, Power Bars, water, etc. Continue on Durham-Pentz Rd.

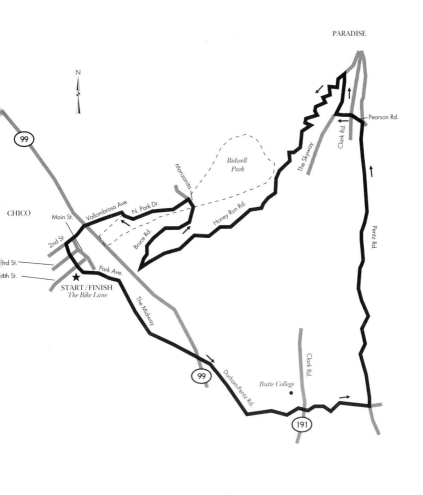

PARADISE

Pearson Rd.

The Skyway

Clark Rd.

Bidwell Park

Manzanita

Honey Run Rd.

Pentz Rd.

CHICO

Main St.

Vallombrosa Ave.

N. Park Dr.

2nd St.

Bruce Rd.

3rd St.

4th St.

Park Ave.

START/FINISH
The Bike Lane

The Midway

Clark Rd.

99

Durham-Pentz Rd.

Butte College

191

N

99

- 18.2 Durham-Pentz Rd. ends at Pentz Rd. Left onto Pentz Rd.
- 19.0 Climb begins.
- 23.8 Paradise city limits; food and water available.
- 25.0 Left onto Pearson Rd.; rollercoaster hills—have fun!
- 28.5 Pearson Rd. ends at The Skyway. Turn right onto The Skyway.
- 28.6 Left onto Honey Run Rd. *Caution:* Steep and bumpy descent on twisty one-lane road. Wear gloves and watch for cars.
- 32.2 Honey Run Rd. widens to two lanes.
- 34.3 Covered bridge at Butte Creek. Veer left and continue on Honey Run Rd.
- 38.7 Right onto The Skyway. Back to civilization.
- 39.5 Right onto Bruce Rd.; Bruce Rd. becomes Manzanita.
- 42.9 Left onto Vallombrosa Ave.
- 43.1 Left onto N. Park Dr.
- 45.4 Swimming hole at "One Mile." Turn right onto Vallombrosa Way; then make an immediate left onto Vallombrosa Ave.
- 46.0 Vallombrosa Ave. becomes 2nd St.
- 46.3 Left onto Broadway.
- 46.5 Ride ends at The Bike Lane, 4th St. and Broadway.

21

Monitor Pass Classic

Woodfords—Markleeville—Monitor Pass—Topaz Lake—Gardnerville, Nevada—Minden, Nevada—Centerville, Nevada—Woodfords

They're out there every weekend. As soon as the snow melts, they're out there.

—Markleeville resident,
overheard in the Tiers of Joy cafe

When you see them all out there, clad in their electric-yellow windbreakers and gnawing on their Power Bars, you have to wonder, "Am I one of them?" Even if you sport the same gear, wear the same clothes, and drink the same powdered substances, there's something about seeing them all out there, sweating up mountains in a majestically pristine setting. It feels a bit funny—like you're not as different as you thought you were.

Are you one of them? The answer, of course, is yes. Anyone who's gone to the extreme of buying this book—and anyone who's even *thinking* about tackling Monitor Pass, the famed Markleeville Death Ride's toughest of five mountain climbs—is one of them.

And while it may seem a bit strange to see all your newfound bikie brothers and sisters out on the same remote roads on a non-century day, it's also a bonding experience. They've all been riding up and down the same mountains that you are going to ride. They have sweated on the same roads. They have grunted around the same steep switchbacks.

This is Alpine County, home of the much-heralded Death Ride, where thousands of cyclists convene once a year to push their limits up five mountain passes and over 130 miles. But since it has received so much press, bicycling in Alpine County is no longer limited to one hyped-up day. Death Riders are out tackling these roads all summer long.

The Monitor Pass Classic charts a formidable and diverse route by starting in Woodfords (also the start-finish of the Diamond Valley Ramble), climbing the toughest of Alpine County's mountain passes, and then traveling onward to Nevada before eventually wending its way back to Woodfords. The actual Death Ride travels over both sides of Monitor as well as Ebbetts, Luther, and Carson Passes. If you dare try all five passes, a detailed map of the area will help you plot the route. Or better yet, sign up for the ride—which fills up fast—by contacting the Alpine County Chamber of Commerce at the number on page 123.

Six miles of rolling hills get you from Woodfords to Markleeville, where cafes, delis, and a general store form a two-block town. Stop in one of the stores and tell the person behind the counter what you're about to do. In other small mountain towns, people would say you were crazy; they'd warn you not to try it. Here they don't bat an eye. They've seen it all before. They understand our kind.

Continuing past Markleeville, you'll begin ascending alongside Monitor Creek at a relatively moderate rate. *Caution:* Don't be tricked into thinking you've begun your climb up Monitor. You ain't seen nuthin' yet. The cilmbing begins in earnest when you turn left at the sign TO MONITOR PASS—and it doesn't let up until you reach the top, 9.6 miles later. In fact, it seems to get harder the higher you go. Is it really getting steeper, or is the altitude beating you down? Or could it be that the never-ending 10 percent grades are crushing your mortal legs?

All of these things would be important were it not for the incredible views your pain affords you. Had you stayed on the porch of the general store in Markleeville (a tempting alternative), you would have missed the lush, high-alpine meadows, the shimmering leaves of aspen, the white, peely bark of the birch, the rough and rocky terrain of the mountain, and the incredible mountaintop vistas of a far-below valley floor stretching from California to Nevada. Had you stayed in Markleeville, you would have missed the thrill of climbing to 8,314 feet—and the ecstasy of a lusciously steep, well-deserved descent.

Shortly after reaching the bottom of Monitor and turning onto Highway 395, you'll pass Topaz Lake and cross the Nevada state line. It's browner and flatter here but fascinating in its own right. Mountains spring up from the flat earth with no trace of a foothill. Signs for places like Sharkey's Casino remind you that you're no longer in California. Bike and Ski Sports, on Highway 395 going north out of Minden, is a friendly and high-tech bike shop specializing in road bikes.

As you turn onto Highway 88, the snowy peaks of the Sierra Nevadas loom larger in the foreground, and before you know it, you're back in California, where everything seems to magically become more lush. More dramatic. More serene. And best of all, from the state line Woodfords is just 6 easy miles away.

The Basics

Start: Intersection of Hwy. 88 and Hwy. 89 in Woodfords.
Length: 71.1 miles
Terrain: Steep mountain climbing, lots of rolling hills; low traffic in California, moderate traffic on Hwy. 395 in Nevada.
Food: General stores in Woodfords and Markleeville; no food from Markleeville to Nevada; many food options in Gardnerville and Minden.
For more information: Alpine County Chamber of Commerce, P.O. Box 265, Markleeville, CA 96120; (530) 694–2475, for information on the Death Ride. Bike and Ski Sports, 1685-B Hwy. 395, Minden, NV 89423; (702) 782–0867.

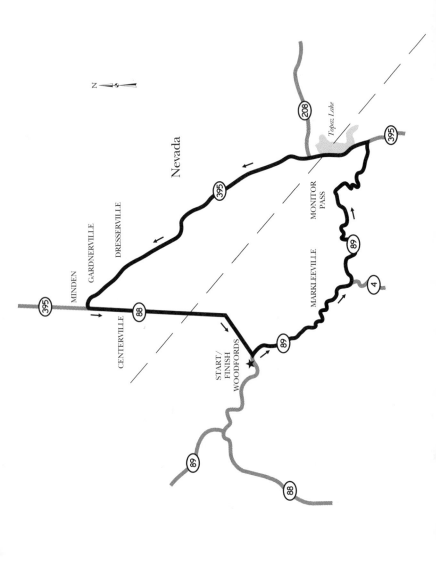

Miles & Directions

- 0.0 From the intersection of Hwy. 88 and Hwy. 89 in Woodfords, turn right onto Hwy. 89 toward Markleeville.
- 6.2 Markleeville city limits.
- 11.4 Left at Monitor Pass.
- 20.0 Monitor Pass.
- 21.6 Enter Mono County.
- 29.3 Left onto Hwy. 395.
- 30.5 Topaz Lake.
- 32.5 Nevada state line.
- 35.7 Intersection of Hwy. 395 and Hwy. 208.
- 54.0 Gardnerville.
- 55.5 Minden.
- 56.9 Left at Hwy. 88.
- 60.3 Centerville.
- 64.9 California state line.
- 70.8 Woodfords city limits.
- 71.1 Ride ends at intersection of Hwy. 88 and Hwy. 89.

22

Diamond Valley Ramble

Woodfords—Diamond Valley—Woodfords

> *A ride is a ride, not a mission, not a race, not an end in itself.*
>
> —Maynard Hershon, *California Bicyclist*

Seems the more you ride, the more you begin to accept suffering into your life as part of the whole cycling deal. You begin to seek out the highest peaks and the ultradistance rides. But in the middle of nowhere, with no hills to worry about, no nervous spasms at the thought of 80 more miles to go, no cars threatening your life as they whiz by at 75 miles per hour, your bike-suffering factor becomes virtually nil. And with hardship out of the way, you are freed up to check out the scenery, savor the quiet—maybe even think deep thoughts, ponder the meaning of life, and so forth. The ride becomes secondary, because it's so carefree that you don't even have to think about it.

While hardcore riders may argue that suffering is precisely the tool necessary to lead body and mind to heights of greatness, the 12-mile Diamond Valley Ramble offers strong evidence that a short, flat ride can, under the right circumstances, be just as beautiful, just as enlightening, as a 150-mile gruelathon.

The Diamond Valley Ramble is the second of two Alpine County rides that start and end in Woodfords and are featured in this book (See Ride 21, Monitor Pass Classic). Along with rustic lodges and cabins aplenty, there are thirteen campgrounds in

Alpine County alone, and even more in the surrounding areas. Facilities range from primitive (a.k.a. fewer people) to fully equipped with showers and flush toilets (read: Winnebagos, kids, Doritos). Spend the weekend here and tackle both the Diamond Valley Ramble and the Monitor Pass Classic, or leave the classic to your more aggressive partners and take to exploring the less-traveled roads of Diamond Valley—there's more to see than what's on this route slip; all you need is a map.

Leaving from Woodfords, your ride starts with a short, steep pitch of road as you climb up Highway 89 to your turnoff at Diamond Valley Road. Once your wheels hit this thin ribbon of tarmac, all cars disappear and the quiet countryside takes over. Get about 1 mile away from Highway 89 and you are utterly alone. There are no campgrounds, no homes—not even an abandoned shack. The potent smell of wildflowers wafts through the air as the scenery alternates from pastoral meadows to scrubby bushes and barren hills—all cradled by the sylvan, snow-covered peaks of the Sierra Nevadas. As you ride through on your two-wheeled steed, it all feels very Old West in a Hollywood kind of way. You almost expect to see a pair of rugged pioneers/cowboys crest one of the hills atop their horses.

But you are reminded of the realities of the 1990s when you come across the Hung-a-Lel-Ti southern band of the Washoe tribe of California-Nevada, at mile 5.2. From outward appearances, these are not the Native Americans of history books or Hollywood movies, but the modern-day victims of a nation that's forgotten them. This barren patch of land is what the government has given them to call home. And there are no tepees and horses, only modest residences and broken-down cars.

As Diamond Valley Road curls around this small reservation, you can alter the published ride by taking Long Valley Road (which becomes Indian Creek Road when you cross the Nevada state line) all the way to the larger Washoe reservation in Dresserville. From there you can hook up with Highway 395, which intersects with Highway 88 in Minden and heads back to Woodfords.

Continuing past the reservation, your route crosses Highway

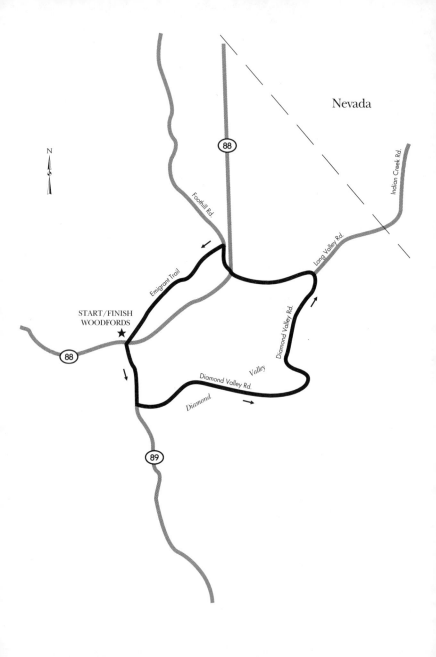

Nevada

(88)

Foothill Rd.

Indian Creek Rd.

Emigrant Trail

Long Valley Rd.

START/FINISH
WOODFORDS
★

Diamond Valley Rd.

(88)

Diamond Valley Rd.

Valley

(89)

Diamond

N

88 and leads to yet another stone-quiet section of riding along Emigrant Trail, a paved road that follows a small portion of the historic route forged by the bold travelers of California's gold rush of 1848. The road rolls along the foothills of the Sierra Nevadas, delivering you all the way back to Woodfords. There you can pick up a snack at the general store and enjoy the serenity of life in the mountains of Alpine County, California's least populated—and perhaps most beautiful—county.

The Basics

Start: Intersection of Highway 88 and Highway 89 in Woodfords.
Length: 12 miles.
Terrain: Mostly flat; some rolling hills; virtually carless roads.
Food: General store in Woodfords; no food available on ride.
For more information: Alpine County Chamber of Commerce, P.O. Box 265, Markleeville, CA 96120; (530) 694–2475. Bike and Ski Sports, 1685-B Hwy. 395, Minden, NV 89423; (702) 782–0867.

Miles & Directions

- 0.0   From the intersection of Hwy. 88 and Highway 89 in Woodfords, turn right onto Hwy. 89 toward Markleeville.
- 0.5   Left onto Diamond Valley Rd.
- 5.2   Hung-a-Lel-Ti, southern band of Washoe tribe of California-Nevada.
- 7.4   Cross Hwy. 88 to Foothill Rd.
- 8.2   Left onto Emigrant Trail.
- 11.3   Right onto Hwy. 89 (unmarked).
- 11.7   Woodfords city limits.
- 12.0   Ride ends at junction of Hwy. 88 and Hwy. 89.

23

Winters Farmland Cruise

Davis—Putah Creek Road—Winters—Davis

> *O beautiful for spacious skies,/For amber waves of grain,/For purple mountain majesties/Above the fruited plain!*
> —Katharine Lee Bates, "America the Beautiful"

Flat. As a pancake. As a desert plain. As a lovebug on your windshield. Flat. Dead Flat. The Winters Farmland Cruise is undoubtedly the most level ride in this entire book. The roads on this tour undulate about as much as a starched shirt on Wall Street.

But this ride is far from flat in terms of scenery. Hellaciously hot in the summer and enshrouded with fog in the winter, the roads around Davis provide a gateway into America's heartland. You'll pedal right past those oft-heralded amber fields of grain with a backdrop of majestic purple mountains outlining the distance.

The ride begins in downtown Davis, a small agribusiness/college town just down the road apiece from Sacramento. As close as it is to sprawling Sacramento, the city of Davis is no suburb. It has a funky, collegiate feel, complete with espresso bars, vegetarian restaurants, and bikes galore. And due to its pancakelike pavement, many of the bikes you'll see are retro Schwinn cruiser types—embellished with flower-laced handlebar baskets—used mainly for the purpose of commuting about town.

From the ride's start at Wheelworks Bike Shop, you'll take to tree-lined Russell Boulevard, which in the summer provides a touch of shade from Davis's unrelenting heat. But cover from the rays in only a temporary luxury. Within 2 miles the road yields to vast, open farmland with miles of crops plotted on meticulously tilled land. The rhythm of symmetrically planted rows is eventually broken at mile 7.4 by a stone bridge covered with a blanket of graffiti. With its multicolored rainbows and swirls, this vivacious structure can bring a smile to even the sternest of mouths, giving rise to the argument that maybe sometimes—just sometimes—graffiti can actually be a beautification process.

But after you cross the bridge, it's back to the fields. As you turn onto Putah Creek Road, the often still air and always empty roads—combined with the symmetry of the rows of crops—can feel almost spooky, as if you could be the next victim in a *Children of the Corn* movie or something. If your imagination is running wild, you can amuse yourself otherwise by trying to guess what the farmers are growing. One mile yields leafy little bushes erupting from mounds of brown earth. But pedal another mile and you're passing orchards of almonds and apples growing in carefully planned abundance.

After 14 miles of flat farmland, you'll get a few rollers as you head into Winters. A few, mind you. And certainly nothing to shake a stick at. These are your only "hills" for the day, so make what you will of them. Cross Putah Creek and you're rolling into the farming community of Winters, a small and welcoming town with a few sincere restaurants, a large feed-and-seed store, and less than a dozen blocks of modest homes.

From your Winters vantage point, the distant mountains are drawn nearer. Lofting on the horizon, these peaks are still far enough away that you can enjoy their scenic merits instead of worrying about an impending climb.

A stoic white barn marks your turn onto Road 27—no real need for cutesy names like Almond Orchard Avenue out here. Even the roads are plotted meticulously, forming a series of grids that mirror the crops in between them and making it incredibly difficult to get lost. To get back to Davis, just keep making right turns.

On your way back to Davis, a few barren, twisted trees stand alone in the fields with their branches outstretched like an old witch's hand. Adding to this eerie scene, a run-down mansion is perched awkwardly on the side of the road, marking your final turn onto Road 99 back toward town. The once-regal house seems to be rotting from within, yet it has an obvious psychedelic air coursing through it, as if it's now inhabited by Deadheads/UC Davis students.

From here you'll have 8 more flat miles back to town. Once in town, you will find that the best latte east of San Francisco and an ollalieberry muffin is available at Espresso Roma, a block from Wheelworks. Park your bike amid the city cruisers for which Davis is noted. Afterward you can mill around in Wheelworks and B & L Bikeshop (right next door at 610 3rd Street). If you're feeling brave, ask the salespeople about another great Davis ride—the Davis Double. If your Winters Farmland Cruise was too easy, you might just love the Davis Double. Sponsored by the Davis Bike Club, this well-attended ride covers 200 miles in one day, and this time you'll make it to those majestic purple mountains. Ouch!

The Basics

Start: Wheelworks Bike Shop, 3rd St. and F St., downtown Davis.

Length: 40.7 miles.

Terrain: Flat, quiet farm roads.

Food: Espresso Roma is at 231 E. St. There's a great selection of restaurants in downtown Davis. Also worth a visit is the Davis Food Co-op at 6th and G Streets. There's a general store in Winters if you need a quick fix.

For more information: Davis Bike Club, 336 Del Oro, Davis, CA 95616; DBC Hotline, (530) 756–0186. B & L Bikeshop, 610 3rd St., Davis, CA 95616; (530) 756–2500. Wheelworks Bike Shop, 3rd St. and F St., Davis, CA 95616; (530) 753–3118.

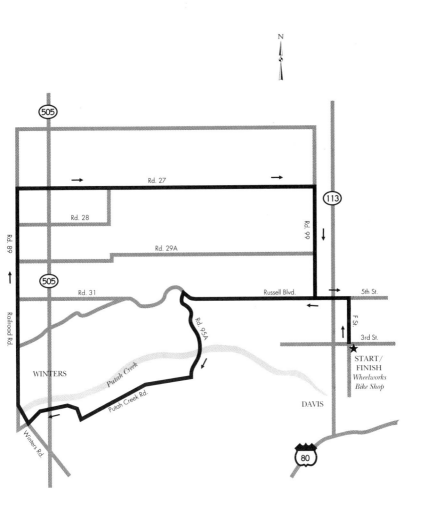

Miles & Directions

- 0.0 Wheelworks Bike Shop, 3rd St. and F St. Go north on F St.
- 0.2 Left onto 5th St.
- 0.6 UC Davis. Fifth St. becomes Russell Blvd.; bike path available.
- 1.7 Cross over Hwy. 113.
- 6.6 Bike path ends at three-way intersection; sharp left onto Rd. 95A, unmarked.
- 8.0 Right onto Putah Creek Rd.
- 14.3 Cross under overpass; follow sign TO WINTERS.
- 15.2 Right onto Winters Rd.; cross Putah Creek bridge.
- 15.3 Winters. Winters Rd. becomes Railroad Rd. and eventually becomes Rd. 89.
- 22.4 Right onto Rd. 27.
- 23.5 Cross Hwy. 505.
- 32.7 Right onto Rd. 99.
- 36.8 Davis city limits. Rd. 99 becomes Lake.
- 37.9 Left onto Russell Blvd.; bike path available.
- 39.0 Cross Hwy. 113.
- 40.1 Russell becomes 5th St.
- 40.6 Right onto F St.
- 40.7 Ride ends at 3rd St. and F St.

24

Folsom Challenge

*Folsom—American River Bike Trail—Auburn—
Cool—Pilot Hill—Salmon Falls Road—Folsom*

> *A bike God is a talisman. It is something you can only
> get when you are riding. It must be a gift of the journey.
> You can't buy it. You can't know what it is before you get
> it. It just comes.*
>
> —Mark Jenkins, *Off the Map*

In the oft-divisive cycling world, some see bike paths as the
blessed, two-wheeled solution to overcrowded city streets,
whereas others view them as part of a mastermind conspiracy
to keep bicycles off the road. Are bike riders being handed the
recycled rhetoric of the pre-civil rights, down-South, separate-
but-equal dogma? Or do we even *want* to share the roads with
smelly, obnoxious cars?

This ride provides a bit of both. The Folsom Challenge offers
beautiful bike trail, followed by 20 miles of scenic but well-traveled highway, followed by 20 miles of twisting country roads,
before finally returning to the suburbs. Beginning in the Ashland Station Shopping Center, on Greenback Lane and Auburn-
Folsom Road, you immediately are taken away from this busy
intersection and along the beginnings of the American River
gorge. Folsom Dam is on your right, and across the gorge is the
infamous Folsom Prison. At the end of the pavement, at Beal's
Point, there are restrooms and water. This is the upper part of
the Jedediah Smith Bicycle Trail, featured as another ride in this

book. (See Ride 26, American River Bike Trail Ramble.)

The bike path so far has paralleled Auburn-Folsom Road, which you will turn onto at the Folsom Lake Park entrance road. From here you'll have to deal with cars and hills as you make your way to Auburn, but the scenery along the tree-lined road is relaxing, with the white fences of horse ranches bordering the road and the ornate gates of ritzy planned communities popping up every now and then. For most of its length, Auburn-Folsom has a wide shoulder that will serve as a bike lane.

After 20 miles of riding and a thousand feet of climbing, you reach Auburn, a quaint gold rush community now becoming a suburb of Sacramento. Auburn is worth a visit on its own, and a few loops around the downtown section will reveal quite a collection of nineteenth-century architecture. Leaving Auburn on Highway 49, you are immediately plunged into the wilds of the American River canyon. The descent here is smooth, fast, and banked, so save your sightseeing for the bottom, where you are treated to a view of the famous Forest Hill Bridge high above you.

From here there's nowhere to go but up. After following Highway 49 across the American River, you'll be faced with a steep and writhing climb up a skinny road cut deep into the side of the mountain. Shoulders are virtually nonexistent here, and there are a few serious blind spots, so ascend with caution. Although the climb is only 2 miles, the top comes just in the nick of time for most legs. From here the foliage becomes greener and the road transcends from a harsh, mountain-hugging challenge to a rollicking romp through pleasantly rolling fields.

These gentle hills mark your entrance into the tiny town of Cool, where you can get a snack at the general store and be on your way. This blink-and-you'll-miss-it burg boasts beautiful vast pastureland and only a few slight buildings. There's not much to do out here except ride—which, of course, makes the riding near-perfect. You'll roll along for 4 more miles before hitting Pilot Hill and turning off, right after the gas station, onto the unmarked Salmon Falls Road. After dealing with one more brief climb, you'll be treated to miles of luscious, uninterrupted descending through verdant hillsides thick with trees and rust-colored canyons. Gorgeous valley vistas greet you around almost every bend. Salmon Falls Road typifies cycling at its flawless, inspiring best: It's roads like this that renew cyclists' passion for the sport and invigorate our souls.

You'll have 10 miles of countryside before plopping down in the outskirts of Folsom. And at mile 48 you'll pass Folsom Prison—the same one that Johnny Cash made famous with "Folsom Prison Blues," crooning that he "shot a man in Reno, just to watch him die." Don't loiter for long along this stretch of road, lest your intentions be misconstrued by prison authorities. From here it's a quick ride back to the beginning through historic Folsom. At the bottom of the hill on Riley Street is the old town, home of antique shops as well as some interesting restaurants.

The Basics

Start: Ashland Station Shopping Center, Greenback Ln. and Auburn-Folsom Rd. Bicycles Plus, a friendly, high-quality bike shop, is located here.
Length: 50 miles.
Terrain: Steep climbs, lots of rollers and gentle uphill grades, some flat sections; moderate to heavy traffic for 2-mile climb on Hwy. 49 and on Auburn-Folsom Rd.
Food: Coffee Republic, a nice cafe, is at the start. Various stores are located in Auburn. Convenience stores are in Cool and Pilot Hill. Nothing between Pilot Hill and Folsom.
For more information: Bicycles Plus, 6606 Auburn-Folsom Rd., Folsom, CA 95630; (916) 989–9670.

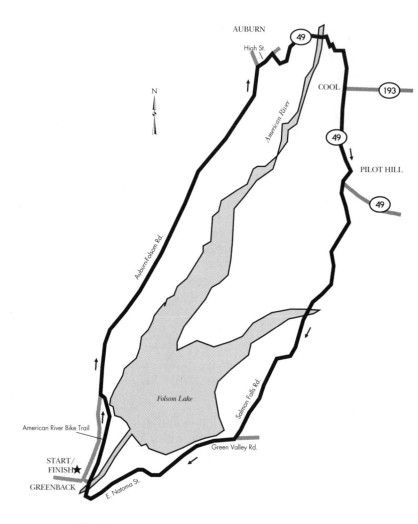

Miles & Directions

- 0.0 Greenback Ln. and Auburn-Folsom Rd., Folsom, Ashland Station Shopping Center. Head toward Folsom on the sidewalk on the north side of Greenback until you reach the American River Bike Path, just before the Rainbow Bridge. Do not cross this bridge.
- 0.1 Left (north) on the American River Bike Trail. Follow the path until you reach Beal's Point.
- 5.4 Bike path veers right to Beal's Point. Restrooms, water available. Turn left on entrance road to Folsom Lake State Recreation Area and leave the park.
- 5.7 Right onto Auburn-Folsom Rd.
- 17.5 Auburn city limits.
- 20.4 Right onto High St.
- 21.4 High St. becomes El Dorado (Hwy. 49); begin twisty descent.
- 23.7 Turn right onto bridge at bottom of descent; follow sign TO COOL.
- 23.8 Begin steep climb.
- 25.7 Summit.
- 27.1 Cool city limits.
- 30.6 Pilot Hill. Go straight past Rattlesnake Bar Rd. and Pilot Hill gas station.
- 31.0 Right onto Salmon Falls Rd. (unmarked).
- 31.1 Left at stop sign.
- 42.8 Right onto Green Valley Rd.
- 45.8 Right onto E. Natoma St.
- 48.0 Folsom State Prison.
- 49.0 Right onto Riley St., which veers left into Greenback Ln. Take care crossing the narrow Rainbow Bridge.
- 50.0 Ride ends at Greenback Ln. and Auburn-Folsom Rd.

25

Calaveras County Challenge

*Copperopolis—Felix—Pool Station—San Andreas—
Angels Camp—Copperopolis*

> *He'd give him a little punch behind, and the next minute
> you'd see that frog whirling in the air like a doughnut—
> see him turn one summerset, or maybe a couple if he got
> a good start, and come down flat-footed and all right,
> like a cat.*
>> —Mark Twain, "The Celebrated Jumping Frog of
>> Calaveras County"

Mark Twain spent only three years of his life in California's
Gold Country, but in that time he put himself and the area on
the map with his first big story, "The Celebrated Jumping Frog
of Calaveras County." And even today people there haven't forgotten him. Everywhere you go, you run into places like the
Mark Twain Mini Mall or the Twain Super Six Movie Theatre. In
Angels Camp frog icons pop up everywhere, an annual jumping
frog contest and festival are still held, and the legend of the
cantankerous genius that was Mark Twain lives on.

The Calaveras County Challenge heads out to the delightful
burg of Angels Camp via some of the finest backroads in all of
California. Starting in the nowheresville town of Copperopolis,
the cycling is immediately rural and peaceful. Along rolling
country roads sit lonely farmhouses plotted on miles of open
space. Oak trees with branches arching lazily toward the earth
spring from the folds of the hills, and solitary cows graze in pas-

toral bliss amid the vast open fields.

As you meander through the hilly countryside, cars and houses become fewer and farther between, and roads with no names or signs are common, making it easy for the first-time bike tourist to get confused. The trickiest section comes when you reach the small cluster of farmhouses at mile 6.8. Your main road seems to veer off to the left, but you should continue straight past the farms. You'll be heading toward the hills on a road so jarring that you can feel every crack and cranny of its broken asphalt. This portion of the route is a part of the epic Copperopolis Road Race, which is held each March, starting in Milton. As an additional side trip, you can retrace the race's route by circling the Salt Spring Valley Reservoir on Salt Spring Valley, Hunt, and Rock Creek Roads. Thankfully, the surface improves as the first real climb begins, at mile 8.8 on Hunt Road. As you twist upward through the countryside, the soft outline of the Sierra Nevadas appears on the horizon and all the heart-pounding agony seems worthwhile.

As you drop down to Pool Station, you'll turn off onto Pool Station Road, where golden wildflowers blanket the soft hills for much of the year and the branches of oak trees swoop down to shade the road on hot summer days. Another 2-mile climb awaits you at mile 23.4, and the terrain becomes more rocky as you pass a jagged reservoir before summitting and heading downward to the town of San Andreas. Here you'll find numerous food options and B&Bs, making it a great place to take a break—or the perfect home base for a weekend of bike exploring.

Leaving San Andreas, you'll want to avoid Highway 49, which is narrow and heavily traveled. Instead, take the back way on Calaveritas and Dogtown Roads. Here is one of the most picturesque roads in Calaveras County. You will travel through a series of small canyons and divides, past deserted mining towns and old rambling ranches that seem to have been there forever.

Dogtown Road ends at Angels Camp, where you can relive all the Twain lore, visit a nineteenth-century schoolhouse, and groove to the Old West atmosphere that permeates the historic downtown. You'll definitely want to venture past highway 4 and check out the historic old town, which is just a few miles down the main road. When you've had your fill, turn around and head back to Highway 4, where you'll have a hilly 10 miles back to Copperopolis.

The Basics

Start: McCarty's Copper Inn, Copperopolis, located off Hwy. 4, which can be accessed from Hwy. 5 in Stockton. McCarty's is a gas station, convenience store, and deli.

Length: 60 miles.

Terrain: Rolling roads, with some extended climbing; mostly quiet backroads with little traffic; some rough surfaces.

Food: McCarty's Copper Inn has energy bars and myriad other snacks to get you started. You won't have another chance to refuel until you reach San Andreas at mile 28.8.

For more information: Calaveras County Chamber of Commerce, 3 North Main St., San Andreas, CA 95249; (209) 754–4009. McCarty's Copper Inn, 522 Main St., Copperopolis, CA 95228; (209) 785–2500. The Mountain Peddler, 352 S. Main St., Angels Camp, CA 95221; (209) 736–0771.

Miles & Directions

- **0.0** From McCarty's Copper Inn turn left onto Main St. toward Hwy. 4.
- **0.5** Cross Hwy. 4; go straight on Rock Creek Rd.
- **6.6** Road Ts; turn right onto Salt Spring Valley Rd.
- **6.8** Straight past unmarked road, then through gate, past farmhouses toward hills.
- **8.8** Salt Spring Valley Rd. intersects with Hunt Rd., then becomes Hunt Rd. Continue straight and begin climb.
- **12.2** Begin descent.

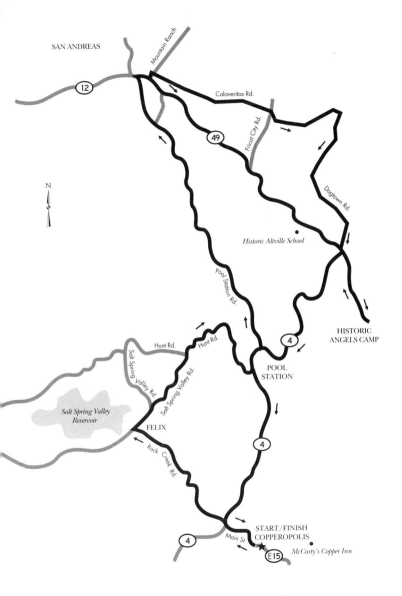

- 12.5   Left onto Hwy. 4.
- 13.2   Left onto Pool Station Rd.
- 23.4   Begin climb.
- 25.3   Summit.
- 28.8   Right onto Hwy. 49 (unmarked); San Andreas.
- 29.2   Left onto Mountain Ranch, past the hospital.
- 29.7   Right on Calaveritas Rd.
- 34.7   Right on Fricot City Rd.
- 34.8   Left on Dogtown Rd.
- 46.3   Left on Hwy. 49 to Angels Camp.
- 48.3   From Angels Camp, left onto Hwy. 4 west to Copper-opolis. (Mileage varies here, depending on how far into town you went.)
- 59.5   Left onto Main Street in Copperopolis.
- 60.0   Ride ends at McCarty's Copper Inn.

26

American River Bike Trail Ramble

Old Sacramento—Fair Oaks—Folsom—
Fair Oaks—Old Sacramento

The bicycle is its own best argument. You just get a bike,
try it, start going with the thing and using it as it suits
you. It'll grow, and it gets better and better and better.
—Richard Ballantine, *Richard's Ultimate Bicycle Book*

In the midst of one of America's major metropolitan areas lies 31 miles of parkway bike path that promises many pleasant rides to cyclists of all levels. This is the American River Bike Trail, which goes from Old Sacramento along the Sacramento River to Beal's Point on Folsom Lake.

Formally known as the Jedediah Smith Bicycle Trail, the final leg of the bike path was completed in 1985. But much earlier a similar trail ran along the river to Folsom. Built in 1896 by the Capital City Wheelmen, this path was in its day a wildly popular cinder track. Although it eventually fell into disuse, the American River Bike Trail was resurrected in 1967 as part of the American River Parkway. The bike trail is now an integral part of one of the largest metropolitan parks in America.

There are many places to access the bike trail, but we will start in the most picturesque—Old Sacramento, a restoration of the town during the gold rush. Consisting of about one hundred buildings built between 1849 and 1876, Old Sac now also features numerous coffee shops and restaurants that make it a good place to begin and end a ride. For those inclined to tour without a bike, Old Sacramento also has the wonderful California Railroad Museum and the Discovery Museum, a museum of science and natural history.

From Old Sacramento, the bike trail heads north through Discovery Park, passing over the American River on the Discovery Park Bridge. This bridge once stretched between Oakland and Alameda Island in San Francisco Bay and was removed piece by piece to its present site in the 1920s.

Throughout its length, the bike trail is two lanes and roughly 10 feet wide, with dirt paths for runners and equestrians on either side. Mileage markers are painted on the trail, starting at Discovery Park. Speed limits on the bike path are 15 mph, and since roughly half a million cyclists ride the trail each year, this is a speed we would recommend, particularly on summer weekends.

Leaving Discovery Park, the trail goes west through a vast area of dense blackberry brambles, towering valley oaks, and fields of star thistle. On your left, behind the blackberries, is an archery complex. On your right, in the distance, is the Sacramento skyline. And you can almost imagine a time when huge forests of cottonwood and valley oak lined the American River.

Farther on you will pass ponds and sloughs populated by beaver, deer, heron, and ducks. This relatively unspoiled natural area manages to coexist only a few minutes from the city and provides interesting nature-watching in any season.

Leaving behind these large wild areas, the trail passes by the Campus Commons Golf Course and reaches Sacramento State University. If you are planning a shorter ride, this is a good place to stop. The Cobblestone Cafe across from the Guy West Bridge on University Avenue offers a varied menu in pleasant outdoor surroundings. To return from here, it is possible to shortcut back through the city (take M Street once you cross the J Street underpass). Downtown Sacramento is a very bike-friendly town to ride in with wide, shady streets and lots of bike lanes.

The trail, however, continues another 20 miles before reaching Folsom Lake. Goethe Park at mile 15 has water and bathrooms. At mile 20, in Fair Oaks, riders can cross the Bridge Street Bridge and take a short side trip into old Fair Oaks.

Past Fair Oaks, the parkway is lined with dredge tailings from the days of hydraulic mining. It then passes the Nimbus Fish Hatchery and crosses the river on the Hazel Avenue Bridge to run along the north side of Lake Natoma, until finally reaching the town of Folsom, another potential place to stop.

After the Rainbow Bridge at Folsom, the trail finally begins to climb a bit, and the pavement ends at Beal's Point in another 4 miles. On this section, riders should stop to admire the beginnings of the American River gorge and to contemplate the massive Folsom Prison on the other side of the river.

One nice thing about the Jedediah Smith Trail is that it is accessible in dozens of places, and several easy rides can be started in Folsom, the Nimbus Hatchery, Fair Oaks, Goethe Park, Sacramento State, or Old Sacramento. The trail is always a great place to take kids and offers them plenty of natural entertainment as well as places to stop and eat.

The Basics

Start: Old Sacramento, along the river in downtown Sacramento. Ample parking is available.

Length: 64 miles if you ride the entire trail out and back, but this route can be divided into many smaller rambles.

Terrain: Flat except for the last few miles to Folsom Lake. Some bicycle traffic.

Food: Many interesting restaurants are located in Old Sacramento. At Campus Commons, across the Guy West Bridge from Sacramento State, is the Cobblestone Cafe. Fair Oaks and Folsom offer a variety of restaurants and convenience stores.

For more information: The Rest Stop, 3230 Folsom Blvd., Sacramento, CA 95816; (916) 453–1870. The Rest Stop has a good map selection, including the official American River Park-

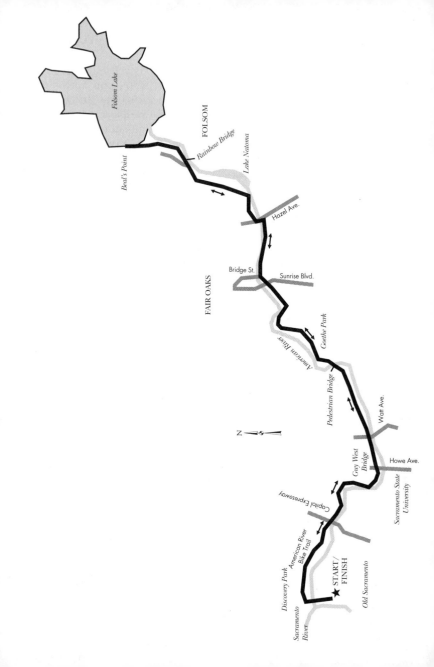

way map. Sacramento County Parks; (916) 336–2061. American River Parkway Foundation; (916) 456–7423.

Miles & Directions

- 0.0   Old Sacramento. Follow the American River Bike Trail north along the Sacramento River.
- 1.0   Cross the Discovery Park Bridge. Loop to the left underneath the bridge. You are on the bike trail. This is where the painted mileage markers begin.
- 3.5   Cross Northgate Blvd.
- 8.0   Pass Campus Commons Golf Course.
- 9.0   Pass the Guy West Bridge. (To return to Old Sacramento directly, cross the bridge, turn right on the levee trail, and follow it to J St. Take J St. through the underpass, and turn left on 56th St. for a block. Turn right on M St. Right on 35th. Left on L St. Right on Alhambra for a block. Left on K St. Left on 14th for a block. Right on L. Left on 9th for a block. Right on Capitol Mall. This route is known as "Generic" by locals.)
- 15.0   Goethe Park.
- 21.0   Fair Oaks Bridge. This is a pedestrian bridge.
- 24.0   Nimbus Fish Hatchery. Cross the American River on the Hazel Ave. walkway.
- 29.0   Rainbow Bridge at Folsom.
- 32.0   Beal's Point. To return to Old Sacramento, follow directions in reverse.

27

Forest Hill Classic

Forest Hill—Middle Fork of the American River—
Rubicon River—Big Trees Park—North Fork of the
American River—Forest Hill

Bike riding helps develop a person's sense of discovery.
—David Perry, *Bike Cult*

Epic is the best word for any ride out of Forest Hill, a Sierra community that straddles the Forest Hill Divide, between two great canyons of the American River. The Forest Hill Classic takes in both these canyons, burying itself in the American Rubicon Gorge and glimpsing the canyon of the American River North Fork. Along the way, it includes one of the most beautiful descents and one of the most wonderful climbs in the Sierras.

The town of Forest Hill is a gold-rush town that is gradually being encroached upon by late twentieth-century civilization (the population has grown to nearly 4,000 people). There is a modern grocery there—Worton's—and it's a good place to stock up, as this will be the only food source you will see. In the summer, this can be a four-water-bottle ride, and since there is only one place to get water after the start, prepare yourself. Remember: Once you leave Forest Hill you will not pass another house of any kind for over 50 miles, and there is substantial climbing along the way.

This ride begins with a huge smile. That's because once you

turn onto Mosquito Ridge, you are descending *up* the Rubi-con/Middle Fork of the American Gorge on one of the world's most beautiful roads for a good 10 miles. In other words, even though you are going downhill, you are also going into the mountains, so as you descend, the walls of the gorge rise above you. For an experienced rider, this can be a brakeless descent—just don't spend too much time looking over the edge at the Rubicon, 2,000 feet below.

Another surprise here. Under normal summertime condi-tions, as you descend you will notice the temperature growing warmer. Forest Hill is at 3,200 feet—the river is at 1,100 or so, and the canyon traps heat. On summer afternoons it is not un-usual for the temperature to be over one hundred degrees.

Mosquito Ridge actually doesn't go all the way to the Rubi-con but bottoms out at Peavine Creek (also called the North Fork of the Middle Fork of the American). You'll probably no-tice a few cars parked along here, as this is a dipping spot for the locals. Afterward, an extraordinary 25-mile climb begins.

After passing Ralston Ridge Road, Mosquito Ridge Road climbs steadily up the north side of the divide between the American Middle Fork and Peavine Creek. Traffic here is nonex-istent, and the scenery is spectacular. On your right are tower-ing cliffs seeping with water, and on your left a vertical drop to Peavine Creek far below.

After 10 miles, the road breaks into the high country and passes the Placer Big Tree Grove, the most northerly grove of the sequoias. This is a good stopping point since it's the only source of water on this route. A tar-and-chip road of about 2 miles leads to a parking lot with bathrooms and water. If you need water, it is either here or from a stream, which is not rec-ommended in the Sierras.

Mosquito Ridge Road is now at over 5,000 feet, and you will notice a lot of alpine flora, including Douglas fir, Ponderosa pine, spruce, and also bear clover, known for its distinctive cre-osote smell. You may also experience some shortness of breath. The grade at this point is not particularly steep, so save your breath. You'll soon need it on the steep grades and gravel of

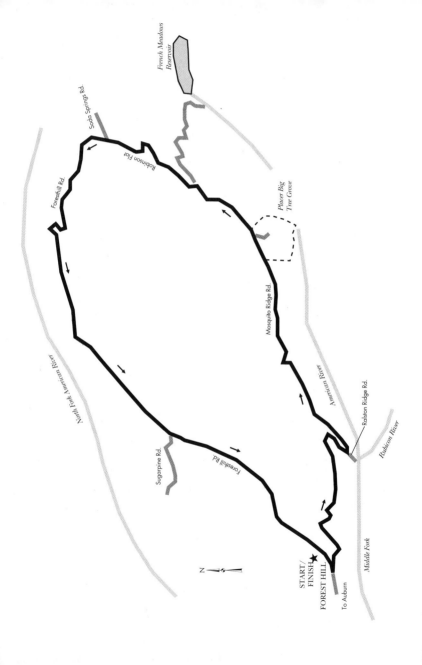

French Meadows Reservoir

Soda Springs Rd.

Foresthill Rd.

Robinson Flat

Placer Big Tree Grove

Mosquito Ridge Rd.

North Fork American River

American River

Sugarpine Rd.

Foresthill Rd.

Ralston Ridge Rd.

Rubicon River

Middle Fork

N

START/FINISH

FOREST HILL

To Auburn

Robinson Flat. Only the very strong and determined will be able to ride this entire stretch without a dismount, but the walking sections are short, and generally the road is quite pleasant.

Robinson Flat tops out at 6,700 feet at the intersection with Foresthill Road. From here it's a swooshing 20 miles of downhill back to the start. If you wish to soak up a little more of that backwoods ambiance, stop for dinner at the Forest House Restaurant in the center of old Forest Hill.

The Basics

Start: Forest Hill, 16 miles east of Auburn, on Foresthill Rd. Park along Foresthill Rd., between the old town and Mosquito Ridge Rd.

Length: 63.3 miles.

Terrain: Prolonged descending and climbing. Roads are very free of traffic and smooth, except for a 5-mile stretch of gravel on Robinson Flat. This ride should be done on a road bike. Heavy tires recommended.

Food: No food on the route. Water only at Big Trees. Worton's Grocery is a good place to stock up before the ride. The Forest House Restaurant is recommended.

For more information: Bicycle Emporium, 483 Grass Valley Hwy., Auburn, CA 95603; (530) 823–2900. The Forest Hill Library; (530) 367–2785.

Miles & Directions

- 0.0 Left on Foresthill Rd.
- 0.3 Left on Mosquito Ridge Rd. Two thousand-foot descent over next 11 miles.
- 26.0 Placer Big Tree Grove. The only place for water on this route.
- 29.8 Left on Robinson Flat. Gravel for 5 miles, sometimes steep.

- 12.0 Pass Ralston Cutoff. Continue on Mosquito. Steady climbing for the next 23 miles.
- 35.5 Left on Foresthill Rd. Start downhill.
- 46.9 Pass Deadwood Rd.
- 54.2 Pass Sugarpine Rd.
- 63.3 Ride ends at Forest Hill.

28

Iowa Hill Challenge

Colfax—Iowa Hill—Forest Hill—Colfax

> *The strongest emotions I have experienced were the result of those days, spent on the high roads or on the hill tops, whence I could see down into the valleys on to the roofs of houses which I felt I could reach and touch with my hand.*
> —Maurice de Vlaminck, *Dangerous Corner*

Got a Triple? You may need one if you plan to do the extraordinary Iowa Hill Challenge. But don't fear stopping, as you are rewarded with a spectacular view of the American River Canyon far below. After this strenuous beginning, The Iowa Hill Challenge offers a varied route that takes you through some of the more interesting mining areas in California, skirts the Alpine highlands, and returns through Forest Hill and the American River Canyon.

The route starts in the old railroad center of Colfax and abruptly descends 1,000 serpentine feet to the American River before beginning the climb up the edge of the canyon wall. For the first 2 miles of this climb, the grade is approximately 15 percent. It's best to stop halfway up for oxygen and to check out the view. You'll probably notice rafting parties in the river below. For long stretches, the hill is about as wide as the back seat of your Dad's old Microbus, so even though you are going at 4 mph, don't plan on much zigzagging.

Just when you are about ready to quit, Iowa Hill tops out

into a beautiful, butterfly-filled stream canyon. It then winds along ridges created by hydraulic mining from the gold rush days, before reaching the town of Iowa Hill, a place untouched by the suburbanization of the California outback. The general store is a welcome stop, but don't expect anything fancy.

Continuing on, the road narrows to one lane of chip and tar as it winds through the alpine country of Strawberry Flat to Sugarpine Reservoir. Douglas fir and Ponderosa pine are common here. This is beautiful, isolated backcountry.

After Forest Hill, Yankee Jim's Road is paved for the first 3 miles then turns to dirt as it winds through American River Ravine. Watch for some spectacular waterfall scenery. At the bridge, there is a swimming spot popular with locals. The descent here is moderately rough but can be done on a road bike with normal tires. The climb is not hard. Yankee Jim's Road turns back to pavement for the last few miles into Colfax. Even though this ride is only 46 miles, it will probably take at least four hours to complete.

If you have some extra energy upon returning, the old town of Colfax is worth exploring. Once a rail center, Colfax is now a quiet, non-touristy, Victorian hamlet a mile or so off the freeway. There are several good restaurants and a health-food store. It's a nice place to take a walk.

The Basics

Start: Park on Canyon Rd., the frontage road on the southwest side of I-80 in Colfax.
Length: 46.5 miles.
Terrain: Very Steep descending and climbing on Iowa Hill. Otherwise rolling. Dirt on Yankee Jim's Rd. Easily done on a road bike. Heavy tires recommended.
Food: Grocery stores in Iowa Hill and Forest Hill. Restaurants in Forest Hill and Colfax. Ruby's Cafe on the northeast side of Hwy. 80 at the Colfax exit is a great eatery.

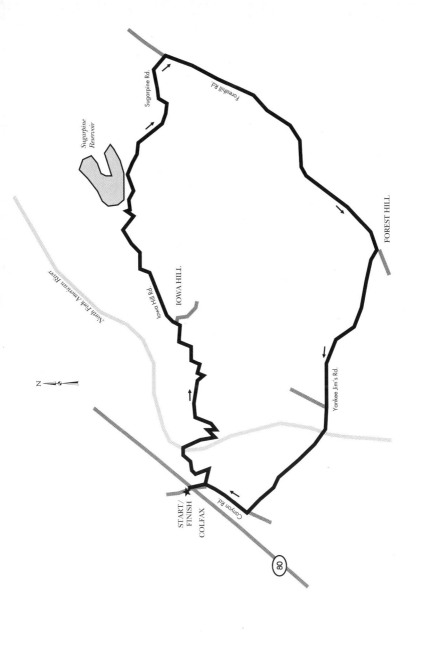

START/FINISH
COLFAX

Canyon Rd

80

North Fork American River

N

IOWA HILL

Iowa Hill Rd

Sugarpine Reservoir

Sugarpine Rd

Foresthill Rd

FOREST HILL

Yankee Jim's Rd.

For more information: Bicycle Emporium, 483 Grass Valley Hwy., Auburn, CA 95603; (530) 823–2900.

Miles & Directions

- 0.0 Colfax Exit of I-80. Take Canyon Rd. southwest following I-80.
- 0.8 Left on Iowa Hill Rd. Steep descent followed by steep climb.
- 10.7 Town of Iowa Hill. Grocery.
- 15.7 Sugarpine Reservoir. Road turns into Sugarpine Rd.
- 23.5 Left on Foresthill Rd.
- 32.4 Left on Yankee Jim's Rd. in Forest Hill. Gravel after 3 miles.
- 45.5 Right on Canyon Rd.
- 46.5 Ride ends in Colfax.

29

Placerville Challenge

Placerville—Georgetown—Placerville

---

*What a joy to pedal into a swirl of colorful leaves raining
down from a shedding red and yellow maple. Or to venture out on a winter's day when the roads are dry but
snow lies on the countryside. It's not the same world you
left in summer; it has its own rewards for those who will
look and listen.*

—Georgena Terry, *The Terry Catalog*

Placerville, formerly known as "Old Dry Diggin's" as well as
"Hangtown," is one of the more charming gold-rush towns in
the Sierra foothills. It is old-fashioned and not too touristy, with
a prosperous Main Street dating from the nineteenth century.
At 1,800 feet, Placerville is, as they say, above the fog and below
the snow. And it is also surrounded by a network of small roads
that, so far, are still above the traffic and provide great riding,
both road and mountain.

Start the challenge in downtown Placerville and ride through
town to get some of the ambiance of the place, as well as some
ideas about where to explore when you return. Once out of
town, the route descends Mosquito Road into the canyon of the
American River, South Fork. This is a descent that requires hard
breaking on a rough road, so take care.

At the bottom you'll find a narrow bridge spanning a rock-
bound chasm with the river rushing through. A steep, multi-
switchback road climbs out, reaching upland meadows and the

community of Mosquito Camp (actually just a few houses).

Descending into the American River Canyon again on Rock Creek Road, the challenge becomes a curvy and thoroughly enjoyable ride. The Rock Creek bridge is a swimming spot favored by locals. Rock Creek Road ends at Highway 193, still a bit above the river. Those who are seeking a shorter ride need to turn left and climb out of the canyon to return to Placerville. For those with the time and inclination, however, turn north into the Eldorado Wilderness.

Here the back-country adventure begins. At the top of the climb on Highway 193, the challenge turns onto tiny Shoofly Road, a real rollercoaster of a road through the pines. At Spanish Flat it crosses a creek valley and then twists into the Eldorado National Forest. Houses become fewer and much closer to the road, as if they have claimed the road as a part of their backyards. Finally, the route enters a national forest campground and leaves habitation behind.

The road at this point is no wider than a bike trail as it climbs up Darling Ridge to over 3,000 feet. Ponderosa pines and other alpine flora appear, as does a vast network of dirt trails. Unless you have a lot of time and a very good map, we don't recommend you take any of these. If you get lost, it's rather unlikely that you'll run into anyone.

Following the pavement, however, you eventually come out on Wentworth Springs Road, which leads to Georgetown, a fairly sizable though isolated Sierra community. Several grocery stores and restaurants can be found there.

To return to Placerville, simply take Highway 193 south. A roaring and safe descent takes you back down the American River Canyon, past Rock Creek and across the river at Chili Bar. For those unacquainted with these types of bars, they are gravel bars on the inside of the river bend. In gold rush days, these were mined for gold, and settlements formed on them. Chili Bar happened to be populated by Chileans. Now it is gone, wiped away by countless floods. But the climb into Placerville is still there: It's a good 1,000 feet with some ten percent grades.

After this ride, you'll probably want to visit one of Placerville's restaurants. Powell Brothers Steamer has wonderful clam chowder and special pan roasts (a seafood stew). You should also check out the Placerville Hardware next door, said to be the oldest hardware store in the West. If you are looking for coffee, The Coffee House, in the unique Soda Works Building, is a few blocks down the street.

The Basics

Start: Downtown Placerville. There are parking lots on Main St.
Length: The short loop is 21 miles. The long loop is 55 miles.
Terrain: Steep descending on Mosquito Rd. Moderately hard climbing on the back roads. Some light traffic on Hwy. 193.
Food: Powell Brothers Steamer on Main Street in Placerville. Several grocery stores are in Georgetown.
For more information: El Dorado County Chamber of Commerce, 542 Main St., Placerville, CA 95667; (530) 621–5885. Golden Spoke Bike Shop, 679 Placerville Dr., Placerville, CA 95667; (530) 626–8370.

Miles & Directions

- 0.0 Main St. and Hwy. 49, Placerville. Go east on Main St.
- 1.0 Left on Mosquito Rd. Take care on the downhill.
- 8.5 Left on Rock Creek Rd.
- 15.5 Right on Hwy. 193.

(For the short loop, left on Hwy. 193, left on Hwy. 49 in Placerville. Distance: 5.5 miles.)

- 17.0 Right on Shoofly Rd.
- 21.0 Right on Spanish Flat.
- 21.5 Right on Traverse Creek, called FR 11.
- 24.5 Right on Bear Creek Rd./FR 11. This becomes Darling Ridge/FR 11.

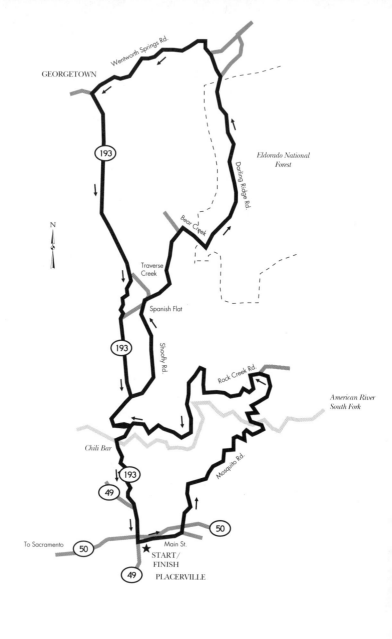

GEORGETOWN

Wentworth Springs Rd.

193

*Eldorado National
Forest*

Darling Ridge Rd.

Bear Creek

Traverse
Creek

Spanish Flat

193

Shoofly Rd.

Rock Creek Rd.

*American River
South Fork*

N

Chili Bar

193

49

Mosquito Rd.

50

To Sacramento

50

Main St.

★ START/
FINISH

49

PLACERVILLE

- 33.0 Right on Balderston Rd.
- 34.0 Left on Wentworth Springs Rd.
- 38.5 Georgetown. Left on Hwy. 193.
- 50.0 American River crossing at Chili Bar.
- 54.5 Merge left on Hwy. 49 in Placerville.
- 55.0 Ride ends in Placerville.

30

June Lake Loop Ramble

June Lake—Silver Lake—Grant Lake—
Mono Lake—June Lake

> *Birth, copulation and death. Fine. In truth, however,*
> *there were at least two other things in which Amanda*
> *strongly believed. Namely: magic and freedom.*
> —Tom Robbins, *Another Roadside Attraction*

Tucked away from the barren, Road Warrior-esque landscape of Mono Lake lies a verdant and lush triad of lakes cradled by alpine granite. Just past the desolation of Highway 395, there's an outcropping of summer fun waiting to be had on the June Lake Loop Ramble. Kids on rafts, anglers with their hip boots and fishing poles, and moms cooking up barbecues dot the shores of the ever-inviting Silver Lake. But while the area is well used and populated with resorts, it is not overused. Somehow the June Lake Loop has remained a relatively quiet and composed destination. Add to that a pristine alpine setting, inviting swimming holes, and gentle open roads, and you've got a dreamy place where the riding is easy and the living is good.

Traveling by two wheels is a great way to experience all this area has to offer. And you'll find lots of good reasons to stop along the way, be it to watch a deer leaping across the road, to cool your sweaty body in the lake, or to check out the unreal-looking, brilliantly colored rock formations that rise eerily from the still water of Mono Lake.

The ride begins at the junction of Highways 395 and 158 and immediately climbs up the charmingly named Oh! Ridge before dropping into the resort town of June Lake. From here the terrain presents few challenges as the road travels along the shores of each lake. Keep in mind, however, that the altitude never drops below 8,000 feet, so even though there aren't any major climbs, there is a good reason for that nauseated, out-of-breath, general bummer of a feeling you may be experiencing.

If you can get past altitude problems and are able to enjoy the scenery, you'll find glimmering lakes; waving, peeling birch trees; and cascading waterfalls. As you near Grant Lake, the lush scenery transforms to a desolate moonscape of jagged lake and barren hills—a foreshadowing of sights to come at Mono Lake.

After 16 miles on the tranquil June Lake Loop Ramble, you'll be faced with a decision. You can either turn around and retrace your path, or you can venture out on busy Highway 395, which isn't nearly so peaceful but does afford some cool views of the wonderfully curious Mono Lake—a sight worth beholding. And if you take Highway 395, there's even a side road (mile 16.5) you can follow out for 5 miles to check out Mono Lake's South Tufa.

Either way, you can't go wrong—these 22 or 32 miles combine some of the best elements of bike riding into one neat package—the luxury of beautiful terrain; the freedom of gentle, less-traveled roads; the magic of mind-expanding sights; and the satisfaction of a good workout.

The Basics

Start: June Lake Loop Rd., southern end, at intersection of Hwy. 395 and Hwy. 158.
Length: 22 or 32 miles.
Terrain: Rolling hills to flat. Less traffic on Hwy. 158; more traffic on Hwy. 395. Not advisable in winter months.

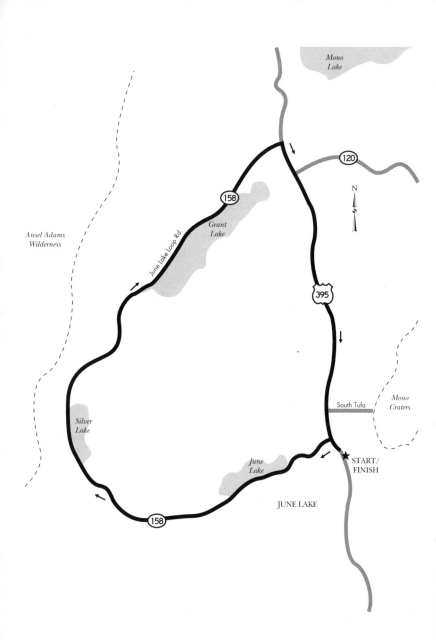

Food: There's a general store at the ride start, plus restaurants and stores, mostly situated in June Lake, as you travel around the loop.

For more information: Mammoth Lakes Ranger Station, P.O. Box 148, Mammoth Lake, CA 93546, (760) 934–2505.

Miles & Directions

- 0.0 June Lake Loop Rd., southern end, at intersection of Hwy. 395 and Hwy. 158; take Hwy. 158 (June Lake Loop Rd.).
- 0.7 Begin climb.
- 1.1 Oh! Ridge.
- 2.4 June Lake city limits.
- 6.5 Silver Lake.
- 11.1 Grant Lake.
- 15.0 Mono Craters.
- 16.0 Hwy. 158 intersects with Hwy. 395; right onto Hwy. 395.

Option: You can turn around at the intersection and retrace your path on the less traveled June Lake Loop Rd. for a total of 32 miles.

- 16.5 Mono Lake, South Tufa turnoff option (will add 10 miles to total).
- 22.2 Ride ends at intersection of Hwy. 395 and Hwy. 158.

31

Glacier Point Classic

Yosemite Valley—Chinquapin—
Glacier Point—Yosemite Valley

> *Yosemite Valley, to me, is always a sunrise, a glitter of*
> *green and golden wonder in a vast edifice of stone and*
> *space.*
> —Ansel Adams, *The Portfolios of Ansel Adams*

If ever there was a climb that was worth the agony, it is the excruciating and unyielding grind up to Glacier Point, which rests high above the Yosemite Valley. Atop Glacier Point the halting views of Half Dome and Yosemite Falls seem like a miracle, and all the possibilities of the world become magically apparent. When your knees start quivering at the Glacier Point vista area, it won't be the 25 miles of climbing that's causing you to shake in your cleats—it'll be the striking, mystical, tear-evoking view.

Your road to nirvana begins in the hub of Yosemite Valley mayhem, where tourists from every corner of the globe clamber through aisles of souvenir T-shirts, visors, and snow domes. Most of these people will never make it past the crammed campgrounds and snack bars of the valley, and as with any road to enlightenment, the steps (or pedalstrokes) you take away from the masses are the ones that mark your pathway to greatness. It seems like the tougher the journey, the greater the rewards.

And so your route winds out of the valley and begins the harrowing, daunting climb to Glacier Point. Be forewarned: In order to endure this ride, you've got to have a bit of sado-masochism in your blood. It's just that hard. Another info-nugget: No matter how hot it is in the valley, bring a windbreaker. You'll be traveling from the valley floor at around 4,000 feet to 7,214 feet.

At mile 8.3 you get your first glimpse of views to come and also an opportune excuse to stretch your legs when you reach the Tunnel View, where the valley and its surrounding mountains lie before you in all their glory. The Wawona Tunnel is about a mile long with a sidewalk and lights. This is where bikes should go. The tunnel roadway is one lane each direction and heavily traveled. Forge ahead for another 8 miles and you'll reach Chinquapin, a town that doesn't seem to have a population but does at least have a store where you can take a break and load up on snacks and whatnot. From here you've got another 14 uphill miles through alpine birch and past huge slabs of granite en route to the granddaddy of all granite formations: Half Dome.

Two miles from the vista area, you'll summit the climb and be treated to a steep and winding descent. Then, at mile 32.3, you can finally dismount your bike, wobble off to a bench on your noodley legs, and soak up the natural wonders of Yosemite—an experience heightened by rushing, pumping endorphins. And when you finally get to the top, dripping and exhausted, you can say "ha!" to all the car drivers up there. They think you're a maniac, they think you're sick—but you know better. You know what they're missing.

The Basics

Start: Yosemite Valley Visitor Center in Yosemite Village, accessible via Hwy. 120 or Hwy. 140.
Length: 64.8 miles.
Terrain: Steep, extended mountain climbing; some high-traffic areas; most advisable on weekdays in the fall or spring. Road closed in winter.

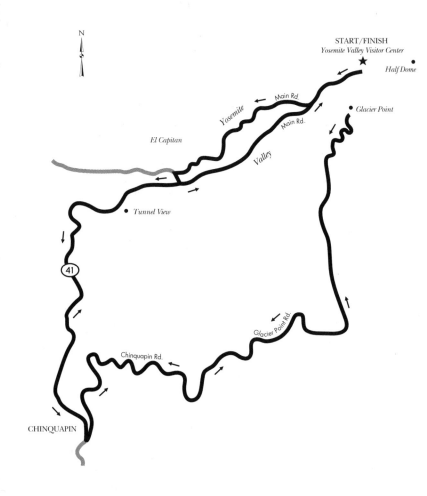

N

START/FINISH
Yosemite Valley Visitor Center

Half Dome

Glacier Point

Main Rd.

Main Rd.

Yosemite

El Capitan

Valley

Tunnel View

41

Glacier Point Rd.

Chinquapin Rd.

CHINQUAPIN

Food: Stock up on food-on-the-fly at the Yosemite Village grocery store. There's a store in Chinquapin that might be open, but other than that you're on your own. Bring as much water as you can possibly carry. This is a ride on which you need to be completely self-sufficient.

For more information: Public Information Office, P.O. Box 577, Yosemite National Park, Yosemite, CA 95389; (209) 372–0265.

Miles & Directions

- 0.0   Yosemite Valley Visitor Center; follow signs TOWARD PARK EXIT.
- 0.3   Veer right onto Main Rd.
- 5.7   Left onto Hwy. 41. In the park this is called Wawona Rd. The sign here will say "Wawona Fresno." Cross the Pohono Bridge. Begin climb.
- 6.7   Right onto Hwy. 41 to Glacier Point.
- 8.3   Tunnel View. Take the sidewalk through the Wawona Tunnel.
- 16.2 Left onto Chinquapin Rd. (becomes Glacier Point Rd.).
- 30.3 Begin steep descent!
- 32.3 Half Dome and Glacier Point; turn around and retrace path back to Yosemite Valley.
- 64.8 Ride ends at Yosemite Valley Visitor Center.

Central Coast

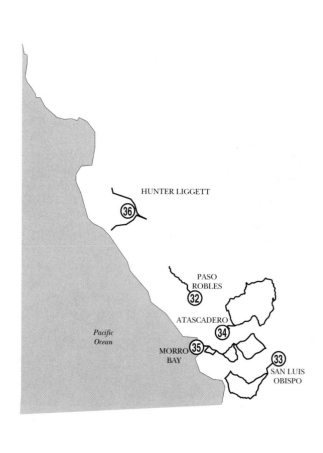

HUNTER LIGGETT

36

PASO
ROBLES

32

ATASCADERO

34

*Pacific
Ocean*

MORRO **35**
BAY

33

SAN LUIS
OBISPO

Central Coast

32

Lake Nacimiento Classic

Paso Robles—Nacimiento Lake—San Antonio
Reservoir—Lockwood—Paso Robles

> *Whenever I'm alone, I tend to brook,/but when I'm not*
> *out on my bike, it's a different mood./I leave my brain*
> *at home, get up on the saddle./No hangin' around, I*
> *don't diddle-daddle.*
>   —Luka Bloom, "The Acoustic Motorbike"

There's a Denny's restaurant right off Highway 101 in the
smallish town of Paso Robles. And there's a nice guy who's
working there and saying his life isn't going anywhere 'cause
he's stuck in this po-dunk town.

If only that guy had a bike.

Paso Robles may not exactly be a kickin' destination loaded
with entertainment value, but the landscape is fertile and
inviting and cleansing. Wide-open roads lined with almond
and walnut trees curve through the hills to Nacimiento Lake.
Vineyards and farmlands spread from quiet country roads and
give you the space and freedom to think, to regroup and re-
discover the possibilities of life and the world. Corny? Perhaps. But ask the myriad bicyclists who take to these roads
why they ride here. You're likely to get a similar answer.

The Lake Nacimiento Classic dives into the unexplored
farmland of the Central Coast, an area with so many back-

roads and so few cars that you'll feel like you've gone to road bikers' heaven. Keep in mind, however, that the Central Coast is extremely hot in the summer, and shade is a precious commodity on many of these roads, making spring and fall the best times to plan a ride.

The rolling road out to Nacimiento Lake is filled with cyclists and marks the first part of your journey. To make this ride a cruise instead of a classic, you could head out to the lake, do some recreating, and then simply turn around and head back to Paso Robles. If you continue on from the Nacimiento Lake Resort, North Shore, you'll be faced with a steep climb that eventually drops you down into a virtually deserted stretch of vast, flat open land. You probably won't run into too many bicyclists out here. It's the kid of place where you're more likely to encounter a tractor than a car.

As you move near the Lockwood city limits at mile 40.3, you move away from the barren plains and back into the fertile, tree-covered hills surrounding Nacimiento Lake. While making the transition back to greenness, gnarled, barren trees stand stoically next to more prosperous ones, posing a question mark—as if to cast some uncertainty on the promise of fertility rendered by the ever-deepening vibrancy of the terrain. Just as you think you've successfully flown from the barren fields, you pass another twisted dead tree.

But as you climb amid the oaks and continue upward through the woods, an unmistakable verdancy returns. You can almost taste and feel the richness of the soil, the bounty of the lake. After nearly 12 miles of tough climbs, you are treated to incredible views from high above the San Antonio Reservoir, which sparkles below and marks your return back to Paso Robles.

From the reservoir you'll be connected once again to the undulations of Lake Nacimiento Road, and you can glide back to town tired from the long miles and tough climbs but refueled both mentally and physically.

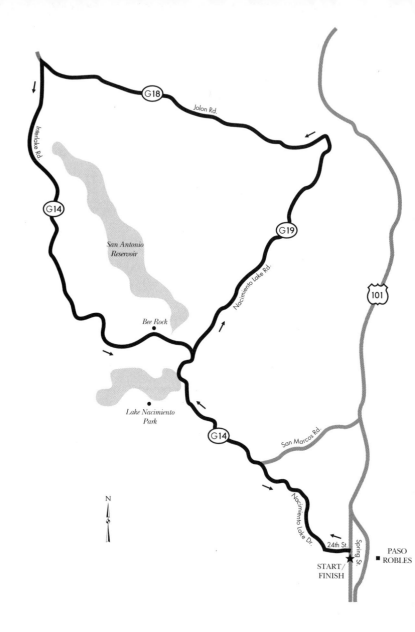

The Basics

Start: Paso Robles (off Hwy. 101) at 24th St. and Spring St.
Length: 80 miles.
Terrain: Hilly; steep climbs; some extended flat areas. Open roads; little traffic most of the way. Very little shade.
Food: Stock up in Paso Robles; otherwise, you're limited to the Western Oak Restaurant at mile 29.3, a store in Lockwood at mile 40.3, or the Bee Rock store at mile 57.9.
For more information; San Luis Obispo Bike Club; (805) 543–5973. Sunstorm Cyclery, 6905 El Camino Real, Atascadero, CA 93422; (805) 466–6430.

Miles & Directions

- 0.0 From 24th St. and Spring St., go west on 24th St.
- 0.4 Veer right, following Nacimiento Lake Dr.
- 6.1 Straight past San Marcos Rd.
- 8.1 Right onto Nacimiento Lake Rd. (unmarked).
- 8.2 Begin climb.
- 9.2 Summit.
- 15.8 Right, following G-14 to Lake Nacimiento/San Antonio Reservoir Recreation Area.
- 16.2 Lake Nacimiento Resort, North Shore. Begin steep climb.
- 17.2 Summit.
- 17.5 Straight past Interlake Rd.
- 19.3 Veer right, following Nacimiento Lake Rd.
- 26.4 Left onto Jolon (say *Ho-lon*) Rd.
- 35.5 Straight past New Pleyto Rd.
- 40.3 Lockwood city limits.
- 41.7 Left onto G-14, Interlake Rd.
- 48.2 Begin climb.
- 49.2 Summit.
- 54.7 Begin climb.

- 55.7 Summit.
- 59.2 Begin climb.
- 60.8 Summit.
- 61.2 Lake Nacimiento/San Antonio Reservoir.
- 62.5 Right onto Nacimiento Lake Rd.
- 71.9 Right onto Nacimiento Lake Dr.
- 79.6 Nacimiento Lake Dr. becomes 24th St.
- 80.0 Ride ends at 24th St. and Spring St.

33

San Luis Valley Cruise

San Luis Obispo—Arroyo Grande—Grover Beach—
Pismo Beach—Edna—San Luis Obispo

I owe my soul to each fork in the road, each misleading
sign, 'cause even in solitude, no bitter attitude can dis-
solve my sweetest find.
                        —Poi Dog Pondering, "Thanksgiving"

From a young hipster on a Harley-Davidson to a sun-dried farmer on a John Deere. From a flurry of cafes, bookstores, and restaurants to the wide expanse of an open field. In San Luis Obispo, city and country rub close familial elbows. It's the kind of place where you can ride from the busy, rambunctious streets to serene roads in less than ten minutes. And don't think cyclists haven't figured this out. As soon as you roll out of town, you'll find yourself sharing the road with more cyclists than cars.

Your ride starts on the heavily trafficked streets of downtown San Luis Obispo before heading out to the more countrified Orcutt Road, which weaves through the golden hills of the Central Coast. At Lopez Drive you'll turn left and head toward Arroyo Grande under the shade of lush oak trees, which soon give way to the area's more typical amber hills. When you finally emerge from the countryside and find yourself in the seaside town of Arroyo Grande, it's just a 4-mile ride to Highway 1, where the Pacific Ocean spreads out before you and expands the possibilities of the world in a way those inland hills never could.

But after a short jog along the beach, your route heads back inland as Price Canyon Road slices through the vast, open countryside. And when you hit Highway 227, you're home free—it's an easy 6 miles back to San Luis Obispo. There you can patronize one of the myriad hip cafes and ponder the virtues of both city and country, of both rolling, fertile farmland and endless ocean. Because in San Luis Obispo, you don't have to choose; you can have it all.

The Basics

Start: Downtown San Luis Obispo, accessible via Hwy. 101.
Length: 32.6 miles.
Terrain: Rolling hills; mainly quiet roads, some busy sections.
Food: There's a health food store right on the route in Pismo Beach, along with whatever else your heart desires. There are also plenty of options at the ride start/finish in San Luis Obispo.
For more information: San Luis Obispo Bike Club; (805) 543–5973. Art's Cyclery, 2140 Santa Barbara St., San Luis Obispo, CA 93401; (805) 543–4416.

Miles & Directions

- 0.0 From Higuera St. and Broad St., go left (south) on Broad St.
- 1.5 Left onto Orcutt Rd.
- 2.3 Veer right at stop sign, following Orcutt Rd.
- 3.3 Left at stop sign, following Orcutt Rd.
- 10.9 Lopez Water Treatment Plant.
- 11.5 Right onto Lopez Dr. to Arroyo Grande.
- 14.2 Straight past Huasna to Arroyo Grande.
- 15.0 Arroyo Grande city limits. Lopez Dr. becomes Huasna Rd.

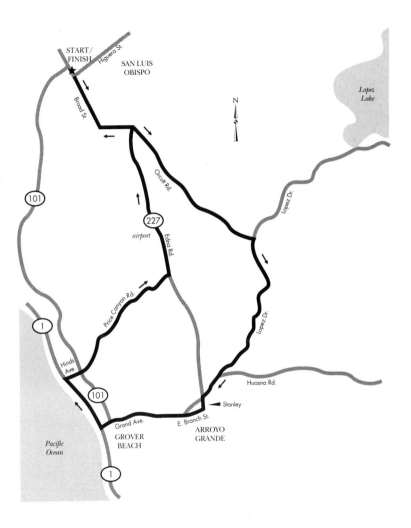

- 15.8   Left onto Stanley; road becomes E. Branch St.
- 16.1   Downtown Arroyo Grande.
- 16.8   Cross Hwy. 101; road becomes Grand Ave.
- 19.5   Right onto Hwy. 1.
- 21.0   Right onto Hinds Ave.
- 21.2   Cross Hwy. 101; road becomes Price Canyon Rd. This stretch of road is narrow and can be fairly busy.
- 26.1   Left onto Hwy. 227 to San Luis Obispo.
- 29.5   San Luis Obispo airport.
- 30.7   San Luis Obispo city limits. Hwy. 227 intersects with Orcutt; becomes Broad St.
- 32.6   Ride ends at Broad St. and Higuera St.

Oak Ridge Challenge

Atascadero—Morro Bay—Cayucos—Santa Rita
Ridge—Oak Ridge—Templeton—Atascadero

Those green-robed senators of mighty woods,/Tall oaks,
branch-charmed by the earnest stars,/Dream, and so
dream all night without a stir.

—John Keats, *Hyperion*

Atascadero is a funny little city, punctuated by quaint farm-houses, an old-style town square, and new-style strip malls. But get out of town—which takes only about 3 miles of pedal-ing—and you quickly catapult yourself into the throes of na-ture. Oak trees dripping with moss reach down to brush your face, quiet ranches nestle among rolling hills, and at times you hear nothing save the rush of the wind.

The Oak Ridge Challenge encompasses all this and more. The delight begins at mile 6.2, when you're treated to the vir-tually carless Old Morro Road. This venerable cracked road wends through the shaded sanctuary of a deeply wooded landscape. Rejoining Morro Road (and cars) at mile 7.9, you'll have nearly 12 miles of effortless descending as you twist through the woods and down to the beachfront town of Morro Bay.

As you drop into town, you can see above the often-foggy bay to the limitless blue distance extending outward with the Pacific Ocean. Down in Morro Bay you can't get this perspec-tive, and the town feels creepy—almost mystical—as the towering Morro Rock looms hazily in the forefront, casting its stony presence over the town.

After a few miles along the coast, the route turns back inland again, and before long you're back to the solitude of a hilly forest of moss-draped oak. Only this time there's a bit more challenge. The pavement ends. You hit dirt. Loose gravel. This will be your traveling surface for the next 9.7 difficult, hilly miles. And while these miles can be ridden on a road bike, you may want to consider using a hybrid or mountain bike on this ride to better tackle the loose-gravel, uphill climbing.

As you ascend through the hills and thicker into the woods, all signs of civilization disappear. There are no cars or homes. Expect to see only the deer and squirrels that inhabit the forest. Or perhaps a fairy underneath a mushroom cap: The deeper you ride in, the more you become a part of this world and all the magic that surrounds it. The summit of Santa Rita Road yields a powerful, windswept view of soft hills peeling off into the distance, as well as the narrow dirt road that will lead you back to civilization.

When you're reunited with asphalt, you'll have approximately 10 easy miles back to Atascadero, including one particularly fun stretch of rollers on Templeton Road. When you get back to Atascadero, you can slide off your bike and onto the inviting lawn of the town square, where the ride ends.

The Basics

Start: Atascadero town square, W. Mall and Fountain Way, accessible via Hwy. 101. Sunstorm Cyclery is only a block from the start/finish on El Camino Real.
Length: 50.4 miles.
Terrain: Hilly. Many extended climbs; rough roads, including 9 miles of loose gravel.
Food: There's a large grocery store on El Camino Real right before your turn onto Hwy. 41; there are also plenty of quaint

restaurants in Morro Bay, including a good selection of seafood joints at Fisherman's Wharf; after Morro Bay, you're on your own. At the start/finish you might want to check out the Gourmet Coffee Shop in the Rancho-T Motel.

For more information: San Luis Obispo Bike Club; (805) 543–5973. Sunstorm Cyclery, 6905 El Camino Real, Atascadero, CA 93422; (805) 466–6430.

Miles & Directions

- 0.0 W. Mall and Fountain Way. Go south on W. Mall to El Camino Real.
- 0.1 Left onto El Camino Real.
- 2.8 Right onto Hwy. 41W to Morro Bay.
- 6.2 Left onto Old Morro Rd.
- 6.4 Begin climb.
- 7.3 Summit.
- 7.9 Left onto Morro Rd. (Hwy. 41W).
- 19.1 Morro Bay city limits.
- 19.5 Cross Main St.

Option: For a scenic tour of Morro Bay that'll add 19.7 miles to this tour, follow the directions for the Morro Bay Ramble, page 190, which starts and ends on Main St. and Hwy. 1.

- 19.6 Under Hwy. 1 to beaches.
- 20.8 Pacific Ocean; turnaround point.
- 22.0 Left onto Main St.
- 23.9 Get onto Hwy. 1 at Yerba Buena St.
- 24.3 Cuyana city limits.
- 25.1 Right onto Old Creek Rd.
- 25.3 Begin climb.
- 26.7 Summit at Whale Rock Reservoir.
- 30.0 Right on Santa Rita Rd. For a longer but completely paved route, continue on Old Creek Rd. to Hwy. 46, turn right on Hwy. 46 and proceed to Vineyard Dr.

- 31.2 Pavement ends; loose gravel for 9.7 miles. Rideable on a road bike with heavy tires by an expert rider.
- 34.6 Begin climbing.
- 36.6 Summit.
- 40.4 Left onto Santa Rita Rd.
- 40.8 Right onto Vineyard Dr.
- 41.4 Cross Hwy. 101; road becomes Templeton Rd.
- 41.9 Right onto Templeton Rd.
- 47.6 Sharp right, following Hwy. 41 across Salinas River Bridge.
- 47.7 Atascadero city limits.
- 47.8 Right onto Sycamore Rd. (Hwy. 41).
- 48.9 Left, following Hwy. 41 (Capistrano Hwy.).
- 50.1 Capistrano Hwy. becomes W. Mall.
- 50.4 Ride ends at W. Mall and Fountain Way.

35

Morro Bay Ramble

Morro Bay—Los Osos—Morro Bay

You don't need a weatherman to know which way the wind blows.
—Bob Dylan, *Subterranean Homesick Blues*

Morro Bay stretches eerily along the fog-enshrouded shores of the Pacific Ocean. A string of inviting inns hug the rocky beachfront for just a few short miles, until the end of town is marked abruptly by a monstrously large rock peeking above the fog line and standing solidly in defiance as waves crash chaotically around it. Beyond the ocean one has only to venture a few miles inland before encountering the sun-drenched fields that are characteristic of much of the inland Central Coast.

The Morro Bay Ramble is a rollicking tour, from the eerie, uncertain atmosphere of the coast to the sunshiny promise of golden fields. The ride begins at the towering formation of Morro Rock, part of a string of volcanic peaks stretching along the Central Coast and dubbed the Seven Sisters.

A 2-mile roll through town brings you to Morro Bay State Park, located right on the edge of the sailboat-dotted bay. Tall pine trees and slippery, waxy eucalyptus shade your journey as languid waves lap up against the marshy shores of the bay. And it's not until you turn onto Los Osos Valley Road at mile 7 that the fog disappears and the air dries up with the warmth of the sun.

The 3-mile stretch on Los Osos Valley Road is laden with

traffic but provides a good shoulder for cycling. At mile 10 a flower farm paints the earth with electric tones of orange, pink, purple, and gold and also marks your turn onto one of the most lovely backroads in all of California: Turri Road. This quietly voluptuous road rolls gently upward through green-carpeted hills as it makes its way to Morro Bay. As you ascend through the curving hills, the formidable Morro Rock juts into the horizon and fog begins to roll violently over the hills, marking your return to Morro Bay.

Entering the Morro Bay State Park again, you'll take the steep but short climb up to Black Hill Golf Course before dropping quickly into town and down to Embarcadero Street, where seafood restaurants, crowds, and the trappings of tourism remind you that this isn't *The Ancient Mariner*, but more like the story of the 1990s, where commercialism takes precedence over naturalism. But this little reality jaunt is short-lived (less than 0.5 mile). And, of course, it's not so terribly bad. When you finish the ride in another 1.5 miles, you may find yourself heading back over there for some wharf-style seafood. And that just may be the perfect ending to your alternately sunny and salty ride.

The Basics

Start: Junction of Hwy. 1 and Hwy. 41 in Morro Bay.
Length: 19.7 miles.
Terrain: Rolling hills, some steep pitches, some flat sections. Mostly quiet roads; some heavily trafficked sections on Los Osos Valley Rd. and S. Bay Blvd.
Food: Myriad restaurants in Morro Bay, including the Great American Fish Company and Fat Cat's Cafe, both on Embarcadero St.
For more information: San Luis Obispo Bike Club; (805) 543–5973. Baywood Cyclery, 2179 10th St., Los Osos, CA 93402; (805) 528–5115.

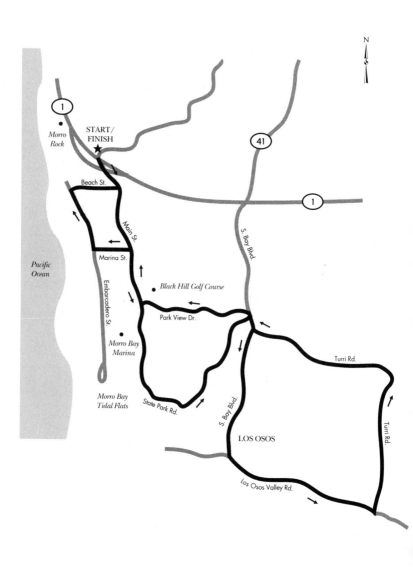

Miles & Directions

- 0.0 From Hwy. 41 and Main St., go south on Main St. toward downtown Morro Bay.
- 0.9 Downtown Morro Bay.
- 2.0 Enter Morro Bay State Park; proceed straight past road to golf course.
- 2.6 Morro Bay Marina and Bayside Cafe.
- 3.7 Right onto S. Bay Blvd. (unmarked).
- 5.5 Los Osos city limits.
- 7.0 Left onto Los Osos Valley Rd. Baywood Cyclery is two blocks to the right.
- 10.0 Left onto Turri Rd.
- 14.9 Right onto S. Bay Blvd.
- 15.8 Morro Bay city limits.
- 16.1 Left into Morro Bay State Park.
- 16.3 Veer right onto Park View Dr., climbing up Black Hill to Black Hill Golf Course.
- 17.0 Summit at golf course.
- 17.2 Right out of park, onto Main St.
- 18.0 Left onto Marina St.
- 18.1 Right onto Embarcadero St.
- 18.5 Right onto Beach St.
- 18.8 Left onto Main St.
- 19.2 Cross under Hwy. 1; continue straight on Main St.
- 19.7 Ride ends at Main St. and Hwy. 41.

36

Hunter Liggett Challenge

Fort Hunter Liggett—Big Sur—Fort Hunter Liggett

> *The bicycle is a curious vehicle whose passenger is also its engine.*
> —John Howard, *The Cyclist's Companion*

On the edge of the Ventana wilderness, Fort Hunter Liggett rests in faded glory. At headquarters, a few cars are parked in the huge lot. An occasional helicopter flies over. The beige barracks, sixty years old and now vacant, speak of busier times. But left behind are some great roads to cycle on, free of traffic and located in an unique natural environment in the highlands behind Big Sur.

The ride starts at the fort headquarters on Mission Road, near Mission San Antonio, and consists of two out-and-back rides through the upland valleys of the Santa Lucia Range. We will treat these as two separate rides since they pass through the same starting point.

Our first ride starts on Del Venturi Road and immediately fords the San Antonio River on a shallow paved ford. Don't be tempted to ride here as the middle is slippery, and the current just strong enough to sweep your wheels out from under you. It's better to remove your shoes and walk across. On a hot summer day, this will be refreshing.

Del Venturi gradually climbs through an oak-studded valley until there is another paved ford of the San Antonio River. After this, you leave Hunter Liggett and enter the Los Padres

National Forest, and soon the road starts climbing seriously. Be aware that you are now crossing open range and can expect some rather wild-looking cattle to be lounging along—and sometimes on—the road. Give them a wide berth.

With more climbing (to around 2,200 feet), you reach The Indians, an area where Indians farmed in the late missionary period. This area features a large sandstone outcropping known as Wagon Cave. Across the road is Junipero Serra, the tallest peak in the Santa Lucias, at 5,844 feet.

A brief descent brings the route to the turnaround at the end of the paved road. This is Memorial Campground, a Forest Service campground where there is no drinking water. Beyond are 18 miles of dirt road, rough but rideable with a road bike. An epic loop would be to take this route to Carmel and return through Big Sur on Highway 1—all in all, 150 miles of riding on spectacular roads.

Returning to Hunter Liggett, the second out-and-back takes Nacimiento Fergusson Road. through Stony Valley, one of the most beautiful isolated valleys in California, filled with huge valley oaks in grassy meadows. Interestingly, all the trees here are fully mature giants. The absence of smaller trees is probably due to overgrazing and drought.

Entering the canyon of the Nacimiento River, the road steepens through numerous switchbacks until the ridge is reached at 2,000 feet. This section is shady and wet, with many live oaks hanging over the road. There is drinking water at the lower campground, Ponderosa.

The ridge top presents the adventurous rider who does not wish to immediately turn around with two difficult but enticing alternatives. First, Cone Peak Road, a dirt road on the right, climbs 1,500 feet toward Cone Peak (5,155 feet). This is a very strenuous climb on a road bike but offers magnificent views of the Pacific. Second, Nacimiento Fergusson abruptly descends to the ocean, with several decreasing radius corners, where all you can see ahead is the Pacific, 1,000 feet below. And, if you choose this way, what you descend, you must also climb.

Finally, there is the easiest alternative: You can turn

around and roll back toward your starting point, enjoying those specimen oaks along the way.

The Basics

Start: Fort Hunter Liggett, Mission Rd. and Del Venturi Rd. Hunter Liggett can be reached on Jolon Rd. from King City. Call (408) 386–2503 to make sure all the roads in the fort are open.

Length: 38 miles and 34 miles.

Terrain: Gradual climbing on Del Venturi Rd. and Milpitas Rd. Some cattle grates and cattle. Very little traffic. Two river fords. Somewhat more traffic on Nacimiento Fergusson Rd. Steep climbing to the ridge at Cone Peak Rd. Steep descending.

Food: Bring your own food and water. There is water at Ponderosa Campground.

For more information: Fort Hunter Liggett road closure information; (408) 386–2503. Los Padres Forest Service; (408) 385–5434.

Miles & Directions

Ride 1:

- 0.0   Mission Rd. and Del Venturi Rd. Parking is available at the fort headquarters. Follow Del Venturi.
- 0.5   Ford of San Antonio River. Slippery!
- 7.0   Second ford of San Antonio River. Slippery!
- 8.0   Left on Milpitas Rd.
- 12.0   Enter Los Padres National Forest.
- 16.0   The Indians, Wagon Cave.
- 19.0   Memorial Campground. Turn around.

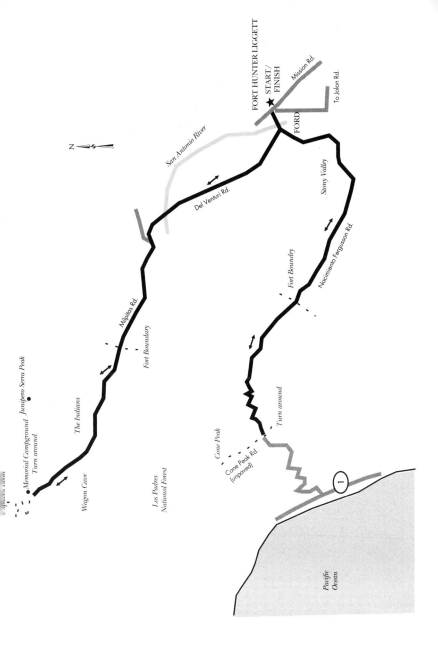

Ride 2:

- 0.0 Mission Rd. and Del Venturi Rd. Parking is available at the fort headquarters. Follow Del Venturi.
- 0.5 Ford of San Antonio River. Slippery!
- 1.0 Left on Nacimiento Fergusson Rd.
- 5.0 Stony Valley.
- 9.5 Leave Hunter Liggett, enter Los Padres National Forest.
- 10.5 Ponderosa Campground, water.
- 17.0 Reach summit at Cone Peak Rd. Turn around. It is 7 miles and 2,000 feet down Nacimiento Fergusson Rd. to Hwy. 1.

Appendixes

A surprisingly large amount of literature is devoted to the sport of cycling. The following titles and club listings only begin to scratch the surface of what's out there, but they do provide a good starting place for learning more about the various aspects of the sport. To really hook into California's vast cycling network in three easy steps, you should: 1. Join a local cycling club; 2. Read *Cycle California!* religiously; and 3. Plan to complete at least one organized cycling event this year.

Regional Cycling Magazines

Cycle California!
P.O. Box 283
Mountain View, CA 94042
(650) 961–2663

Cycle California!, the successor publication to *California Bicyclist,* is the end-all-be-all source for bicycling news, events, and information in California. *Cycle California!* publishes a complete calendar of events that is invaluable to anyone interested in cycling—recreational, touring, racing, or otherwise. You can get the magazine free at most bike shops, or purchase a subscription for $15.

NCNCA Newsletter
19870 Soulsbyville Rd.
Soulsbyville, CA 95372
(209) 532–7785

Devoted exclusively to racing, the Northern California/ Nevada Cycling Association Newsletter is available in a few selected bike shops. It is the only source for the complete racing calendar, road and off-road. Subscriptions are $12/year. Write NCNCA Newsletter, 509 Mota Dr., Bay Point, CA 94565.

Recommended Reading

California Dream Cycling, Bodfish, Bodfish Books. Bodfish, aka Chuck Elliot, has a special feel for the high country.

Cycling the California Outback, Bodfish, Bodfish Books. Bodfish, aka Chuck Elliot, really gets into the outback.

Effective Cycling, John Forester, MIT Press. Tips for urban riding and for improving safe riding practices and skills.

How I Learned to Ride the Bicycle, Francis Willard, Fair Oaks Publishing. An American suffragette in the early 1900s tells of her experiences learning to ride "the wheel."

Off the Map: Bicycling Across Siberia, Mark Jenkins, William Morrow and Company. Eloquent and inspirational cycling travelogue—read this to renew your passion and enthusiasm for the sport.

Road to Ride and *Roads to Ride South,* Grant Petersen and John Kluge, Heyday Books. A detailed description of every climb in the greater Bay Area.

Roadside Guide to Bike Repair, Dennis Coello, Warner Books.

Sloane's New Bicycle Maintenance Manual, Eugene Sloane, Simon & Schuster.

Tales from the Bike Shop, Maynard Hershon, Ten Speed Press. A collection of humorous short stories written by one of cycling's preeminent writers.

The Berkeley Guides: On the Loose in California, written by UC Berkeley students in cooperation with the Associated Students of the University of California, Fodors Travel Publications. My trusty companion during the writing of *The Best Bike Rides in Northern California,* this book provides brutally honest travel information covering the entire state of California.

The Complete Book of Bicycling, Eugene Sloane, Simon & Schuster.

The Outer Path: Finding My Way in Tibet, Jim Reynolds, Fair Oaks Publishing. Another great cycling travelogue.

Touring on Two Wheels, Dennis Coello, Nick Lyons Books. Practical information on safe and trouble-free bike touring.

Cycling Maps

These maps were indispensable tools in the making of this book. Perhaps one day Krebs will have maps like these for the entire state!

Krebs Cycle Products, P.O. Box 7337, Santa Cruz, CA 95061
Lake Tahoe/Gold Country Bicycle Map
North San Francisco Bay/Sacramento Bicycle Touring Map
S.F. Peninsula/Santa Cruz Mountains Mountain Biking Map
South San Francisco Bay and Monterey Bay Area Bicycle Touring Map

Cycling Clubs

The easiest way to access cycling clubs is to check the *Cycle California!* web page at http://www.cyclecalifornia.com. Most local clubs are volunteer-based, and contact numbers are subject to change. Below is a listing of a few of the more prominent clubs.

National

League of American Wheelmen
190 West Ostend St.
Suite 120
Baltimore, MD 21230
(301) 944–3399
National cycling club

Bikecentennial
P.O. Box 8308
Missoula, MT 59807
(406) 721–1776
National bike touring organization; publishes cycling maps.

Regional

Almaden Cycle Touring Club
P.O. Box 7286
San Jose, CA 95150
Hotline: (408) 255–7957
A south bay touring club with 900 members. Promotes Tierra Bella Century.

Alto Velo
Al Williams
1785 Balsa
San Jose, CA 95124
The largest USCF racing club in Northern California.

Bay Area Roaming Tandems
Hotline: (510) 803–0363
The largest tandem club in Northern California.

Chico Velo Cycling Club
P.O. Box 2285
Chico, CA 95927
Hotline: (800) 482–2453

(530) 343–8356
Promoter of the Chico Wildflower and many other rides.

Davis Bike Club
610 Third St.
Davis, CA 95616
Hotline: (530) 756–0186
A large touring and racing club. Promoter of the Davis Double.

Diablo Cyclist
P.O. Box 30263
Walnut Creek, CA 94598
An active touring club.

Fremont Freewheelers
P.O. Box 1868
Fremont, CA 94538
A touring club with some racing. Promoter of the Primavera.

Fresno Cycling Club
P.O. Box 11531
Fresno, CA 93773
A large touring club. Promoter of the Climb to Kaiser.

Grizzly Peak Cyclists
P.O. Box 9308
Berkeley, CA 94709
A touring club. Promoter of the Grizzly Peak Century.

Los Gatos Bicycles Racing Club
Barry Gordon;
(408) 395–6611
A large and active racing club. Promoter of Cat's Hill.

Napa Valley Velo
Dave Carr; (707) 747–6511
An active racing club in the Napa area. Promoter of several races.

Sacramento Wheelmen
P.O. Box 19817
Sacramento, CA 95819
A large touring and long-distance riding club.

San Jose Cycling Club
Hotline: (408) 287–SJBC
A large racing club, established in 1939.

Santa Rosa Cycling Club
P.O. Box 11761
Santa Rosa, CA
Hotline: (707) 544–4803
A large touring and long-distance riding club. Promoter of the Terrible Two and the Wine Country Century.

Valley Spokesmen
P.O. Box 2630
Dublin, Ca 94568
A large touring and racing club with more than 700 members. Promoter of the Hekaton, Cinderella, and the Wente Road Race.

Western Wheelers
P.O. Box 518
Palo Alto, CA 94302
A large touring club. Promoter of the Sequoia.

Credits

The quote on page 25 is from *How I Learned to Ride the Bicycle* by Francis Willard, copyright © 1991, Fair Oaks Publishing.

The quote on page 30 is from *Markings* by Dag Hammarskjöld, copyright © 1964, Knopf.

The quote on page 43 is from *My Work and Days* by Lewis Mumford, copyright © 1979, Harcourt Brace Jovanovich.

The quote on page 74 is from an article by Sean O'Faolain that appeared in the June 1958 issue of *Holiday*.

The quotes on pages 108 and 150 are from *Bike Cult,* copyright © 1995, Four Walls Eight Windows.

The quote on page 135 is from *Off the Map* by Mark Jenkins, copyright © 1992, William Morrow.

The quote on page 145 is from *Richard's Ultimate Bicycle Book* by Richard Ballantine, copyright © 1991, Dorling Kindersley.

The quote on page 164 is from *Another Roadside Attraction* by Tom Robbins, copyright © 1992, Ballantine Books.

The quote on page 168 is from *The Portfolios of Ansel Adams* by Ansel Adams, copyright © 1981, New York Graphic Society/Little, Brown.

The quotes on pages 1, 10, 15, 49, 94, 116, and 126 are from various back issues of *California Bicyclist,* San Francisco. All quotes are reprinted with permission of the publisher.

About the Author

Kimberly Grob is the former editor of *California Bicyclist* magazine and regularly contributes to many national magazines, including *Mountain Bike, Velo News, Women's Sports & Fitness, Backpacker, Inside Triathlon,* and *Triathlete.* She is an avid cyclist who dabbles in many aspects of the sport, including touring, mountain-bike racing, triathlon, and bike commuting. Kimberly lives in San Francisco and enjoys dashing through traffic on her mountain bike. She continues to dream of the day when she will be able to track-stand at a two-minute red light and ride as fast as the San Francisco bike messengers.

About the Editor

John Elgart, who revised the second edition, has written for various cycling publications, including *Cycle California!* and *Winning Magazine.* He is an active bicycle racer and a national champion at the masters level. John has been involved in the cycling community as a club organizer, race promoter, and USCF official. He lives in Sacramento with his wife, Linda, who is also a bicycle racer.